Iron and Heavy Guns
Duel Between the
Monitor and *Merrimac*

CIVIL WAR CAMPAIGNS AND COMMANDERS SERIES

Under the General Editorship of Grady McWhiney

PUBLISHED

Iron and Heavy Guns
Duel Between the
Monitor and *Merrimac*

Gene A. Smith

Under the General Editorship of Grady McWhiney

RYAN PLACE PUBLISHERS

FORT WORTH   BOULDER

Cataloging-in-Publication Data

Smith, Gene A., 1963-
    Iron and heavy guns: duel between the Monitor and the
Merrimac / Gene A. Smith
        p. cm. – (Civil War campaigns and commanders series)
    Includes bibliographical references and index.
    ISBN 1-886661-15-4 (pbk)

    1. Hampton Roads (Va.), Battle of, 1862. 2. Monitor (Ironclad)
3. Merrimack (Frigate) I. Title, II. Series.

    E473.2.S65 1996
    973.7'52—dc20   96–27927
                                                        CIP

Copyright © 1996, Ryan Place Publishers, Inc.

All Rights Reserved

2730 Fifth Avenue
Fort Worth, Texas 76110

Printed in the United States of America

ISBN 1-886661-15-4
10 9 8 7 6 5 4 3 2 1

Book Designed by Rosenbohm Design Group

All inquiries regarding volume purchases of this book should be
addressed to Ryan Place Publishers, Inc., 2525 Arapahoe Avenue,
Suite E4-231, Boulder, CO 80302-6720.

SAN: 298-6779

A Note on the Series

Few segments of America's past excite more interest than Civil War battles and leaders. This ongoing series of brief, lively, and authoritative books–*Civil War Campaigns and Commanders*–salutes this passion with inexpensive and accurate accounts that are readable in a sitting. Each volume, separate and complete in itself, nevertheless conveys the agony, glory, death, and wreckage that defined America's greatest tragedy.

In this series, designed for Civil War enthusiasts as well as the newly recruited, emphasis is on telling good stories. Photographs and biographical sketches enhance the narrative of each book, and maps depict events as they happened. Sound history is meshed with the dramatic in a format that is just lengthy enough to inform and yet satisfy.

Grady McWhiney
General Editor

The author would like to acknowledge and thank
J. Nathan Campbell for his assistance with this volume.

CONTENTS

The brief biographies accompanying the photographs
were written by Grady McWhiney and David Coffey.

CAMPAIGNS AND COMMANDERS SERIES

Map Key

Geography

	Trees
	Marsh
	Fields
	Strategic Elevations
	Rivers
	Tactical Elevations
)ɪ(	Fords
	Orchards
— — — —	Political Boundaries

Human Construction

)(	Bridges
┼┼┼┼┼┼┼┼┼	Railroads
	Tactical Towns
● ○	Strategic Towns
□ ■	Buildings
✝	Church
✕	Roads

Military

▬ ▬▬	Union Infantry
▭ ▭	Confederate Infantry
▱ ▰	Cavalry
ⅲ	Artillery
⚑	Headquarters
	Encampments
⬚ ⊥	Fortifications
⎍⎍⎍	Permanant Works
	Hasty Works
	Obstructions
☆ ✴ ✴ ✀	Engagements
━━	Warships
▬◼	Gunboats
▬▬	Casemate Ironclad
▬○▬	Monitor
↺ ⇒	Tactical Movements
➜	Strategic Movements

Maps by
Donald S. Frazier, Ph.D.
Abilene, Texas

MAPS

PHOTOGRAPHS AND ILLUSTRATIONS

Iron and Heavy Guns
Duel Between the
Monitor and *Merrimac*

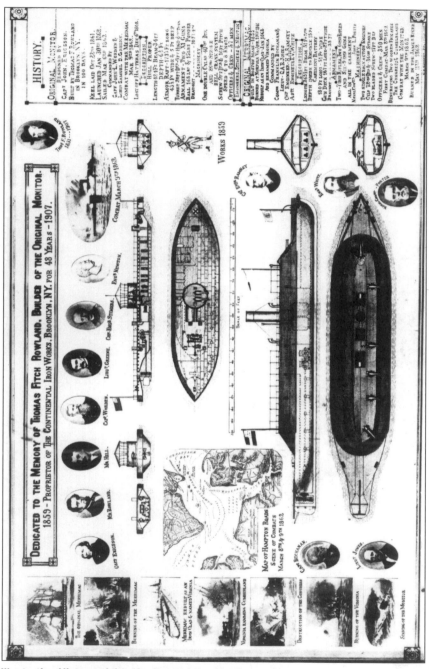

Illustrative History of the *Monitor* and the *Merrimac*

1
"JONES IS NOT OLD ENOUGH"

The forty-one-year-old Welsh Virginian, Catesby ap Roger Jones, sat at the desk in his cramped cabin aboard the C.S.S. *Virginia* (formerly the U.S.S. *Merrimac* and usually known by that name) shortly before midnight on March 8, 1862. He hastily drafted a brief account of the day's events to be forwarded to Captain French Forrest, commander of the Confederate Gosport Navy Yard at Norfolk, Virginia. First-lieutenant Jones, now serving as flag officer owing to his captain having been wounded, nonchalantly claimed that his steam-powered ironclad vessel had left port at 11 A.M. that morning and proceeded down the Elizabeth River to engage Union warships off Hampton Roads, Virginia. During the afternoon his ironclad had sunk the frigates *Cumberland* and *Congress*, driven the steam frigates *Minnesota* and *Roanoke* into shoal waters, and exchanged fire with several small armed steamers and shore batteries. He boasted that only shallow waters and nightfall had prevented the deep-draft *Merrimac* from attacking and destroying other Union warships. At 6:30 P.M. the ironclad had fired her last gun and ninety minutes later had anchored under the Confederate cannon at nearby Sewell's Point. The destruction that lay behind amazed all who had witnessed the day's events; "amid the smoke, and flame, and blood of the last few hours, the centuries-long era of the wooden warship had passed forever." Aboard the *Merrimac*, Lieutenant Robert Minor wrote that "the IRON and the HEAVY GUNS did the work." A new era had been born.

Lieutenant Jones concluded his brief account by reporting that the *Merrimac* had suffered but two men killed and eight wounded during the engagements. After inspecting the condition of his "half submerged crocodile," he described its damage as light. But more importantly, Jones proudly maintained

Catesby ap Roger Jones: Born Virginia 1821; the son of army Adjutant General Roger Jones and nephew of controversial navy officer Thomas ap Catesby Jones, Catesby ap Roger Jones entered the U.S. Navy as a midshipman in 1836; he briefly served under his uncle in the Pacific before embarking on a four-year tour with the East India Squadron; after attending the Philadelphia Naval School in 1841, Jones became a passed midshipman and was posted to the Depot of Charts at Washington, D.C.; thereafter he served on survey duty in Florida, worked in the navy's Hydrographical Office, and again sailed to the Far East; during the Mexican War Jones served in the Pacific and in 1849 was promoted to lieutenant; on a leave of absence in 1851, Jones visited Paris, where he was wounded as an innocent bystander during a riot; returning to duty in 1853, Jones was detailed to ordnance duty at the Washington Navy Yard and assisted John A. Dahlgren in the development of new naval artillery systems, including the Dahlgren Gun; in 1856 he joined the crew of the U.S.S. *Merrimac* as ordnance

that "the bearing of officers and men was all that could be wished." Dead tired, Jones signed and dispatched his report, ate dinner, spoke briefly with ex-Virginia governor Henry Wise and a group of civilians who had gathered on shore, and then tried to catch a few valuable moments of sleep. Little did Jones or anyone else realize that the following day, March 9, 1862, naval warfare would be forever revolutionized as the *Merrimac* confronted the Union ironclad *Monitor* in the world's first modern naval engagement.

Although Catesby ap Roger Jones had unexpectedly gained command of the Confederate ironclad that March afternoon, the lieutenant was not an unlikely candidate for the role he played during those fateful two days. Born at Fairfield in Clark County, Virginia, on April 15, 1821, Catesby was the eldest son of Army Adjutant General Roger and Mary Ann Mason (Page)

officer and developed an intimate knowledge of the ship that would soon fall into Confederate hands to be reconfigured as the ironclad *Virginia*; with the onset of the Civil War, Jones resigned his U.S. commission and was given a captaincy in the Virginia state navy; after participating in an attack on the Norfolk Navy Yard, he was commissioned into the Confederate Navy as a lieutenant in June 1861; Jones worked for a time on the James River defenses, before being named executive and ordnance officer of the C.S.S. *Virginia*, then being transformed into the Confederacy's first ironclad. Jones played a major role in the completion of the ironclad and in recruiting its crew; on March 8, 1862, the *Virginia* ventured into Hampton Roads and attacked the Federal blockading fleet, destroying two wooden warships and threatening still others; during the action, the *Virginia's* commander Flag Officer Franklin Buchanan was wounded and Jones assumed command; the following day Jones commanded the ironclad during its momentous battle with the U.S.S. *Monitor;* although neither vessel could claim a clear victory, the *Virginia* was prevented from doing any further damage to the Federal fleet; passed over for permanent command of the *Virginia*, Jones remained the ship's executive officer until its destruction in May 1862; he later commanded the ironclad *Chattahoochie* and, after his promotion to commander in 1863, headed the Confederate foundry and ordnance works at Selma, Alabama; after the war he pursued business interests and settled at Selma, where in 1877 he was killed in a confrontation with a friend.

Jones (niece of Light Horse Harry Lee, and cousin of Robert E. Lee). The family took extreme pride in its Welsh heritage, as evidenced by Catesby being given the designation "ap" in his name: this is a Welsh prefix meaning "son of," thus Catesby "son of" Roger Jones. That dignity, however, was more deeply seated than the immediate naming of this child after his father. The young man's first name, Catesby, was the same as that of his paternal grandfather, Catesby Jones whom he never met. The name "Roger" could be traced to Roger Jones, the first member of the family to move to Virginia. The acting commander of the *Merrimac* came, in fact, from an old-established, wealthy, and influential Virginia family with strong patriotic ties that would be passed along to its progeny.

The original Roger Jones had emigrated in the 1680s, after serving in the English army and navy under King Charles II. His descendants had continued this warrior tradition. Catesby ap Roger's great-grandfather, Thomas Jones, Jr., had com-

Matthew F. Maury: Born Virginia 1806; Maury studied at Harpeth Academy in Tennessee and entered the U.S. Navy as a midshipman in 1825; he served in the Atlantic and the Mediterranean and sailed around the world aboard the sloop of war *Vincennes*; in 1831 he became a master and sailed the Pacific for three years; returning to the United States in 1834, he published the first of numerous important works, *A New Theoretical and Practical Treatise on Navigation*; promoted to lieutenant in 1837, he was disabled in an accident in 1839 and saw no further sea duty; still, Maury became a prolific contributor to his profession, authoring, under a pen name, several articles that led to much-needed reforms in the U.S. Navy and major improvements in domestic navigation; in 1842 he was appointed to head the Depots of Charts and Instruments at Washington, D.C.; later designated the Hydrographical Office, it was merged with the National Observatory in 1844, with Maury as director of both; a pioneer in the field of

manded a Virginia militia battalion in the Revolutionary War. His father, Roger, had fought the British as a professional army officer in the War of 1812 and ultimately reached the rank of brigadier general. His uncle, Thomas ap Catesby, had joined the Navy and had commanded a flotilla of gunboats against an overwhelmingly superior British force at the Battle of Lake Borgne in December 1814; their sacrifice gained much-needed time for General Andrew Jackson to prepare the defenses of New Orleans. This, in turn, eased Catesby ap Roger's entry into the Navy. In the spring of 1836, his father and uncle appealed to President Jackson for a midshipman's appointment for the boy. On June 18, 1836, Secretary of the Navy Mahlon Dickinson instructed the fifteen-year-old boy to report for duty as a midshipman.

Since that time, Jones had made his mark in the increasingly important scientific and technical branches of the Navy. In 1841, following a three-and-a-half year cruise in the Far

oceanography, Maury examined ship's records and charts to determine the most favorable routes for trans-oceanic voyages; he studied the Gulf Stream, winds, and currents; largely at Maury's suggestion, an international conference was held at Brussels, Belgium, to establish a uniform system for the collection of oceanographic data for use by all nations; in 1855 he published his most important work, *The Physical Geography of the Sea* and later outlined the feasibility of a trans-Atlantic cable; promoted to commander, he resigned his commission in 1861 when Virginia seceded from the Union; several European powers expressed an interest in his services but Maury chose to serve his native state; he entered Confederate service as a commander in June 1861 and was placed in charge of the James River defenses; he worked extensively with torpedoes (mines) and served on the court-martial of Josiah Tattnall following the loss of the ironclad *Virginia*; sent to Europe to further his torpedo experimentation, Maury was also instrumental in procuring and preparing ships for Confederate service; after the war he went to Mexico and served on Emperor Maximilian's cabinet; in 1867 he traveled to England to write and pursue his research but soon returned to the United States; despite offers from numerous prestigious European institutions, Maury accepted a position with the Virginia Military Institute; he continued to write and lecture until his death at Lexington, Virginia, in 1873.

East, he was ordered to the Depot of Charts in Washington, D.C., commanded by Matthew F. Maury. This appointment introduced the officer to naval science and to the brightest minds in the Navy Department, including Virginians Maury, and John M. Brooke. It also allowed him to field-test the latest

John A. Dahlgren: Born Pennsylvania 1809; the son of the Swedish consul at Philadelphia, Dahlgren entered the U.S. Navy as a midshipman in 1826; after service in the South Atlantic and the Mediterranean, he became a passed midshipman in 1832; assigned to the coast survey, he was almost blinded, reportedly after witnessing a solar eclipse; promoted to lieutenant in 1837, Dahlgren endured a five-year recuperation leave; returning to duty in 1842, he served aboard the frigate *Cumberland* until 1845; in 1847 he was assigned, against his wishes, to ordnance duty; this proved a fortunate assignment as Dahlgren devoted his considerable talents to developing new naval artillery systems; he produced plans for several new guns, the most important of which became the eleven-inch Dahlgren Gun; he also introduced iron-carriaged boat howitzers and

greater production capabilities; he was promoted to commander in 1855; when Captain Franklin Buchanan resigned to enter Confederate service in April 1861, Dahlgren became commander of the Washington Navy Yard and as such actively worked to secure the capital; named chief of the Ordnance Bureau in July 1862, Dahlgren also received promotion to captain; elevated to rear admiral in February 1863, he assumed command of the South Atlantic Blockading Squadron in July; he led naval forces in operations against Charleston and in Florida; in December 1864 he aided General William T. Sherman in the capture of Savannah and was present at the occupation of Charleston in February 1865; after the war he headed the South Pacific Squadron and in 1868 again assumed direction of the Ordnance Bureau; relieved at his own request in 1870, he took command of the Washington Navy Yard; Admiral Dahlgren died of heart failure shortly thereafter; he was the author of numerous volumes on ordnance and naval doctrine; his Dahlgren Gun revolutionized naval ordnance and played a major role in the Civil War. His son, Federal Colonel Ulric Dahlgren, was killed during an ill-advised cavalry raid in 1864.

technical advances. From the Depot of Charts Jones moved to the Hydrographical Office, recording magnetical and meteorological measurements, and acquiring scientific knowledge that cleared a path for future appointments.

After another spell in the Far East, Jones spent the period of the Mexican War aboard the ship-of-the-line *Ohio*, most of the time under the command of his uncle Thomas ap Catesby, though without seeing much action. Immediately after the war, he served aboard the steamer *St. Mary*, conducted a thorough survey of the bay at San Francisco, and in May 1849 was promoted to lieutenant. Detached from the *St. Mary* in March 1851, he took a lengthy leave. The leave was prolonged by the effects of an injury he suffered in Paris in December 1851, when he was caught in the street fighting during the coup détat of President Louis Napoleon Bonaparte, who was in the process of turning himself into Emperor Napoleon III. Upon his return home in February 1853, the department ordered Jones to ordnance duty at the Washington Navy Yard—an appointment that would provide his opportunity for the future.

For three years, Jones assisted Lieutenant John A. Dahlgren in experiments on a new type of weapon, the results of which produced the famous "Dahlgren" smoothbore gun. In early February 1856, at Dahlgren's request, Jones was dispatched to serve as ordnance and watch officer aboard the U.S.S. *Merrimac*. For over a year Jones worked with Dahlgren and his guns aboard the *Merrimac* before being transferred to the ordnance steamer *Plymouth* in April 1857. In 1858 he participated as ordnance officer aboard the *Caledonia* in the Navy's Paraguayan expedition, and in 1859 he acted in the same capacity while preparing the *Pawnee* for sea duty.

In a little more than seven years Jones had become one of the most experienced gunnery officers in the Navy. Moreover, he knew more about the new Dahlgren guns than perhaps anyone, besides the inventor. He had become familiar with the operation of the guns both as field pieces, on wheeled carriages, and on the *Merrimac,* on fixed shipboard mountings. It seemed as if destiny had prepared Lieutenant Catesby ap Roger Jones for his place in history.

By the spring of 1861 Jones had been a U.S. naval officer for twenty-five years. He was well established in the naval service, highly esteemed by his peers, and personally popular with his men. But as civil war loomed on the horizon, Jones had a

Stephen R. Mallory: born Trinidad, West Indies, 1812 or 1813; his family moved to Key West, Florida, in 1820 and two years later his father died; an Episcopalian, Mallory attended school in Mobile, Alabama, and, in 1826, the Moravian School for Boys in Nazareth, Pennsylvania; for seven years, he served as customs inspector in Key West before studying law and being admitted to the bar in 1840; he married Angela Moreno in 1838; they had two daughters and three sons, one of whom followed his father into politics; judge of Monroe County, Florida, from 1840

to 1845, Mallory then became collector of the port of Key West; as his legal reputation grew, he became more active in politics; the Florida legislature sent him to the U.S. Senate in 1851 where he served for ten years and was on the Naval Affairs Committee; converted to secession in 1860, he resigned from the Senate when Florida seceded and moved to his home in Pensacola; named Secretary of the Navy by President Davis in 1861, Mallory held that position throughout the war; his department received much less attention than the war department, but unlike the Secretary of War, who was constantly interfered with by the president, Mallory truly commanded the navy, because Davis knew little about naval affairs; Mallory went to England in 1862 and with the aid of naval agent James D. Bulloch planned war cruisers that drove Federal shipping from the seas; Mallory, who experimented with planned economic warfare, refused to allow Confederate naval vessels to become blockade runners; he believed that the Confederates should concentrate their limited resources on ironclads; as conditions deteriorated, he left Richmond with President Davis and was captured in Georgia in May 1865; after his release from prison in March 1866, Mallory practiced law in Pensacola until his death in 1873.

hard decision to make: Would he remain in the old Navy and draw his sword against his family and friends of Virginia; or would he resign his commission and take up arms against the flag under which he had served throughout his adult life? Neither decision would come easy. His father and uncle had faithfully served the Republic, while his great-grandfather and grandfather had fought for their native Virginia during the Revolution.

In the end, Catesby ap Roger Jones placed loyalty to Virginia above loyalty to the Union and on April 17, 1861, he resigned his commission in the U.S. Navy. Not surprisingly, three of his six younger brothers did likewise and took positions in the Confederate Army and Navy. Of his three brothers who remained loyal to the Union, only one fought in the conflict, attaining the rank of brigadier general in the army. On the day following Jones's resignation, Virginia Governor John Letcher appointed him a captain in the Virginia Navy. Less than two months later he participated in an unauthorized attack on the Gosport Navy Yard at Norfolk that captured 300,000 pounds of powder and many shells. After the daring attack Jones was commissioned a lieutenant in the Confederate States Navy on June 10, 1861; he took command of the defenses at Jamestown Island on the James River. For the next five months, Jones oversaw the construction of fortifications and batteries on the island before being instructed to proceed to the Confederate Gosport Navy Yard at Norfolk, Virginia.

On November 11, 1861, Confederate Secretary of the Navy Stephen Russell Mallory appointed Catesby ap Roger Jones executive and ordnance officer aboard the C.S.S. *Merrimac*, then being outfitted as a ironclad warship. The lieutenant had come full circle. He would spend the next four months preparing the former Union ship *Merrimac*—the vessel on which he had served in 1856—for her fateful day against the U.S.S. *Monitor*.

2

"A BURNED AND BLACKENED HULK"

Jones's appointment to the *Merrimac* was somewhat premature. Secretary Mallory had instructed the lieutenant to expedite construction, secure and mount ordnance, recruit a crew, and prepare the *Merrimac* for sea. Yet when Jones arrived at the Gosport Navy Yard that November he found the vessel was far from ready for sea duty. In fact, it was normal that the executive officer would take charge of outfitting a newly commissioned vessel as she prepared for her shakedown cruise. But construction problems and personal controversy between naval constructor John L. Porter and the officer supervising the rebuilding of the ship, Lieutenant John M. Brooke, had delayed her completion and had prompted Mallory to send Jones earlier than anticipated.

The *Merrimac* had been one of six new auxiliary steam-powered forty-gun frigates of 3,500 tons authorized by the Thirty-third Congress and President Franklin Pierce in 1854. Launched from the Boston Navy Yard at Charlestown, Massachusetts, in June 1855 amid the "enthusiastic huzzas" of an estimated one hundred thousand onlookers, she was the first of the class to be completed; and although in her best days she never exceeded seven knots, she was for several years the pride of the U.S. Navy. Immediately after her completion the *Merrimac* served with the West Indian Squadron for a year before being decommissioned for engine repairs in 1857. In September 1857 the frigate returned to service as the flagship of the Pacific Squadron and remained with that station until she was again decommissioned for an extensive equipment overhaul at Norfolk in February 1860. It was this that eventually brought her into the hands of the Confederates when the navy yard was captured from the Union at the outset of the Civil War.

During the morning of April 20, 1861, the commander of the Gosport Navy Yard, Commodore C.S. McCauley, reportedly an insecure, suspicious, meddlesome, heavy drinker, panicked in the bewildering whirlwind of events. He had informed the Secretary of the Navy a few days earlier that Virginia forces had surrounded the Navy Yard and were preparing to attack. Facing such circumstances, he ordered the few loyal U.S. forces under his command to spike the yard's guns and scuttle the ships rather than allow them to be captured.

Only three hours after his men began their task, Captain Charles Wilkes, part of Commodore Hiram Paulding's relief effort, arrived to evacuate the beleaguered Union force. Not perceiving the immediate danger, Wilkes attempted to save the doomed vessels. But failing to salvage the ships, he ordered the vessels completely destroyed to prevent their use by the Confederates. Union troops proceeded to fire the seven ships present, including the 120-gun *Pennsylvania* (supposedly the largest ship in the world at that time) and the steam frigate

Merrimac. For some inexplicable reason Union forces did not set fire to the old frigate *United States,* one of the three original ships of the Navy. Later the Confederates tried to sink the

Charles Wilkes: Born New York 1798; Wilkes entered the U.S. Navy as a midshipman in 1818 and spent most of the next twelve years at sea; promoted to lieutenant in 1826, he was named to head the navy's Bureau of Charts and Instruments in 1830; beginning in 1838, Wilkes commanded a monumental expedition that lasted five years and featured extensive exploration and surveying activities; the expedition surveyed almost three hundred Pacific Islands, thousands of miles of coastline in South America and western North America as well as many previously unexplored sections of Antarctica's coastline, a portion of which bears the name Wilkes Land; the expedition's findings were recorded in numerous volumes, including three authored by Wilkes; an extremely unpopular commander, he was charged with illegally punishing sailors during the expedition and reprimanded; he was nonetheless rewarded with promotion to commander in 1843 and was further elevated to captain in 1855; at the beginning of the Civil War, Wilkes participated in the evacuation of the Norfolk Navy Yard and then assumed command of the steamer *San Jacinto*; thereafter his Civil War service largely consisted of chasing Confederate commerce raiders; in November 1861 he captured the British steamer *Trent*, from which he removed Confederate diplomats John Slidell and James Mason; the *Trent* Affair threatened to bring an aggrieved England to war against the United States but was defused by the diplomatic efforts of Secretary of State William Seward; despite the near-disastrous consequences of his actions, Wilkes was hailed a hero in the North; promoted to commodore in July 1862, he commanded the James River Flotilla and later headed a special squadron that operated against commerce raiders in the West Indies; retired for reasons of age in June 1864, he was promoted to rear Admiral on the retired list in 1866; in addition to his official writings, he authored several other volumes related to his 1838-1843 expedition; Admiral Wilkes died at Washington, D.C., in 1877.

Burning of the Frigate *Merrimac* and of the Gosport Navy Yard

old frigate in the channel below Norfolk; they were unable to cut through the ship's hard live oak timbers.

During the late afternoon Union troops torched the shops and buildings of the yard. The fire that consumed many of the structures also ignited explosive shells and thousands of pounds of powder, making for an impressive fireworks display. But surprisingly, the yard's graving dock (an area used for cleaning and repairing ships' hulls) had not been damaged; over a thousand cannon had not been spiked and two thousand barrels of powder had been overlooked; foundries and forges were untouched; equipment and machinery had not been destroyed; and stores and ships' parts remained intact. Additionally, Confederates later recovered more than 4,000 shells that had been thrown into the river by Union forces. In other words, "it is estimated that the Confederate Government by this blunder came into possession of over $4,000,000 of property, priceless to it in value, and obtainable from no other place."

Before the end of the day Federal forces had supposedly completed their mission and evacuated Norfolk. Only a few hours later Major General William B. Taliaferro's Virginians and Company G, 4th Georgia Infantry, took the Gosport Navy Yard in a bloodless conquest. In many respects it was the most important capture made by the South during the war. In fact, a few days afterwards one Richmond newspaper boldly proclaimed that the yard at Gosport had provided "material enough to build a Navy of iron-plated ships." But most importantly, on the muddy bottom of the adjacent Elizabeth River sat the most significant spoil of the conquest, the burned and sunken hull of the *Merrimac.*

Less than three weeks after the Union evacuation, a naval advisory board recommended to Virginia Governor John Letcher that the *Merrimac* be raised and refitted. The B. & I. Baker Salvage Company of Norfolk had submitted a five-thousand-dollar bid to deliver the vessel into dry dock, and on May

William B. Taliaferro: born Virginia 1822; from a prominent Virginia family, Taliaferro, was graduated from the College of William and Mary in 1841 and studied law at Harvard; he served as a captain in the 11th U.S. Infantry and was promoted to major in the 9th U.S. Infantry during the Mexican War; a Virginia legislator from 1850 to 1853, he rose to the rank of major general in the state militia; following Virginia's secession, he commanded state troops on the Peninsula and entered Confederate service as colonel of the 23d Virginia Infantry in the summer of 1861; serving in Western Virginia, he fought at Rich Mountain and Corrick's Ford; he commanded a brigade in General W.W. Loring's Army of the Northwest (Virginia) and sided with Loring in that general's dispute with General T.J. "Stonewall" Jackson; despite being immensely unpopular with his troops and many fellow officers, Taliaferro was promoted to brigadier general in March 1862 and was assigned, over Jackson's objection, to head a brigade in Jackson's Shenandoah Valley command; he served throughout Jackson's Valley Campaign and during the Seven Days' Battles; in August he assumed command of Jackson's former division during the Battle of Cedar Mountain and led it at Second Manassas, where he was seriously wounded; returning to duty, he played a minor role in the December 1862 Battle of Fredericksburg; denied promotion to major general, he secured a transfer to General P.G.T. Beauregard's Department of South Carolina, Georgia, and Florida; in July 1863, Taliaferro commanded the successful defense of Battery Wagner, near Charleston, that featured a spirited but disastrous assault by the black soldiers of Colonel Robert Gould Shaw's 54th Massachusetts; thereafter Taliaferro held several district commands, assisted in the evacuation of

Savannah, and commanded a division under General Joseph E. Johnston in North Carolina during the final months of the war; although occasionally identified as a major general he was never officially conferred that rank; after the war he practiced law, served in the Virginia legislature from 1874 to 1879 and on the boards of William and Mary and the Virginia Military Institute; General Taliaferro also sat as judge of Gloucester County, Virginia, from 1891 to 1897; he died there in 1898.

30, Captain French Forrest wired General Robert E. Lee that the ship had been resurrected. Forrest, however, was skeptical as he believed that the money and effort needed to renovate that "burned and blackened hulk" would be wasted. As the ship emerged from her forty days in the brackish water of the Elizabeth River, her timbers were charred upward from the waterline and her brass and iron fittings were grotesquely distorted. Nonetheless, Captain Samuel Barron, Confederate commander of naval defenses for North Carolina and Virginia, estimated that even with ruined hull, rusting boilers, and damaged engines, the *Merrimac* was "valued, in her present condition, at not less than $250,000."

In mid-July 1861, Secretary Mallory reported to the Confederate Congress that the *Merrimac* could be rebuilt as a frigate for $450,000. Knowing the parsimonious nature of that body, he also informed Congress that converting the ship into an ironclad would cost only $172,523. Congress instructed Mallory to proceed with the cheaper option and shortly thereafter laborers began a nine-month project of transforming that vessel into a modern ironclad warship.

Although several American entrepreneurs had expressed interest in building an ironclad before the war, the Navy Department had commissioned no such vessel by the spring of 1861. Thus, Confederate and Union ironclads could trace their origins directly to French artillerist General Henri J. Paixhan, who in 1824 had developed the shell gun. Firing a hollow shell filled with powder which exploded on or soon after impact, this weapon rendered even the strongest wooden warships utterly defenseless. The gun's exploding shells splintered timbers rather than bouncing harmlessly off a ship's side. But even with this destructive ability, the weapon did not prove itself during combat until November 1853, almost thirty years later. A few weeks after the beginning of the Crimean War, a Russian fleet armed with Paixhan shells annihilated a squadron of wooden Turkish warships and transport vessels at Sinope. The world took notice as it became obvious that only iron-covered ships could withstand exploding iron shells.

Despite the awsome display of destruction, no country built an ironclad warship until 1859 when Frenchman Dupuy de Lôme introduced a two-hundred-fifty-three-foot wooden steamer, protected by four-and-one-half-inch armor plating. Napoleon III was so enamored with the design of this vessel that by 1861 he had ordered construction of twenty additional iron-sheathed ships. Likewise, the British Admiralty in 1859 also built two ships whose frames and hull were entirely of iron. In fact, the British program was so successful that by 1861 ten ironclads had either been built or were nearing completion, and some had been covered with more than six inches of iron. Meanwhile, in the United States the necessities of war during 1861 forced both the Union and Confederate governments to initiate their own ironclad projects.

Early during the summer of 1861 Lieutenant John M. Brooke had conferred with Secretary Mallory about the possibilities of constructing an ironclad in the Confederacy. The thirty-five-year-old Brooke was one of the most capable officers to secede at the outbreak of the war. He had graduated from the newly established Naval Academy in 1847, invented sounding devices for topographical mapping of the ocean's bottom, and participated in the Navy's North Pacific Expedition and Matthew C. Perry's opening of Japan. Mallory, impressed with the young lieutenant's breadth of knowledge and optimism, instructed Brooke to prepare drawings and calculations for an ironclad ship.

Within days Brooke had completed body, sheer, and deck plans that became the basic model for the Confederate ironclad construction program. Mallory approved the design and assigned naval constructor John L. Porter to draw the details. The secretary also made engineer William P. Williamson responsible for refitting the engines and other machinery. This division of duty ultimately proved cumbersome because Porter would oversee construction, while Brooke would manage the armor and ordnance for the vessel. Meanwhile, Williamson would superintend the ship's machinery. It was inevitable that the boundaries of responsibility would overlap and create controversy. What complicated this process even more was that Mallory instructed Brooke to oversee the entire project. This arrangement produced great resentment between Brooke and Porter that remained for years after the war had ended.

Work had begun on the *Merrimac*'s two-hundred-seventy-five-foot hull even before Congress had voted an appropriation for the project. By mid-July Porter's carpenters had stripped the charred timbers from the hull and eliminated all timbers above the berth deck (about three feet above the ship's unladen waterline). After the damaged boards were removed, as many as 1,500 workmen, often toiling into the night and on Sundays, laid a new gun deck consisting of beams covered by planks from bow to stern. By the end of July the decking had been completed and carpenters prepared to attach the casemated, or bombproof, iron exterior.

Secretary Mallory sent Acting Chief Engineer H. Ashton Ramsay to assist Williamson in repairing the ship's engines. Ramsay was a fine choice since he had been the *Merrimac*'s second assistant engineer before he had seceded. Ramsay claimed that he "knew her every timber by heart." He also understood that the ship's engines were unreliable. During a two-year cruise aboard the vessel, he declared, the engines "were continually breaking down, at times when least expected, and the ship had to be sailed under canvas during the greater part of the cruise." In fact, it was because of the engines that the *Merrimac* had been placed in dry dock at Gosport. Although Ramsay was hesitant to accept his assignment because of his doubts about the engines, he did so after Mallory assured him that the ship would not be sent to any place where her safety might be jeopardized because of engine failure. As engineer, it would be Ramsay's duty to keep the *Merrimac* under power.

Procuring iron for the *Merrimac* soon became Brooke's greatest obstacle. The Tredegar Iron Works at Richmond was the only plant in the South that could supply the necessary metal for the project. Tredegar, founded in 1837, had produced railroad engines and rails and had secured valuable government contracts to supply weapons to the U.S. Navy prior to the Civil War; by 1860 the company had provided the government with more than thirteen hundred cannon. But casting railroad equipment and cannon was much different than rolling iron for plating. The company, virtually overnight, had to transform its operations, train its workmen, and create tools before it could produce the required material.

Additionally, the necessary iron had to be found in order to create the one-inch-thick, eight-inch-wide plating that Brooke desired. More than three hundred tons of scrap iron was gathered from the ruins of the Gosport Navy Yard and sent to Tredegar. Confederate troops scavenged railroad iron from captured Union lines and purchased track from Confederate companies that were too close to the front to operate. By the end of July, one-inch iron plates had been produced and were ready to be shipped to Norfolk.

Brooke had been at Tredegar during the rolling process and personally inspected the finished product. Yet the lieutenant began having second thoughts about the iron's tensile strength when under fire. In early September he sent instructions to the Tredegar mill to start rolling plate two inches thick, of which he would use two layers for the *Merrimac*'s outer shell. This created new complications for the ironworkers. Although they had been able to punch holes in the one-inch plate for the bolts that would anchor the iron to its wooden back, they could not punch holes in the two-inch-plate. Instead the holes had to be drilled, thus increasing costs and greatly slowing production.

While Tredegar nevertheless built up production of the two-inch plating, Brooke retired to Jamestown Island to test samples against the heavy cannon of Catesby ap Roger Jones's batteries. Throughout early October Jones and Brooke tried varying thicknesses of iron layered over a twelve-foot-square wooden target. They angled the targets at thirty-six degrees (the approximate slant of the *Merrimac*'s casemate) and ranged the test guns at 327 yards. They first fired several eight-inch solid iron balls from a columbiad, a chambered cannon that combined qualties of a gun, howitzer, and mortar, at three layers of one-inch plate. The shots shattered the plate and lodged in the wood behind. Brooke and Jones believed this was unacceptable. Next they fired shot from an eight-inch and nine-inch columbiad at two layers of two-inch plating. The balls shattered the outer iron layer, but they only cracked the inner layer; and the wood behind the plating remained undamaged. Jones's official report of October 12, 1861, clearly demonstrated that the *Merrimac* needed the two-inch plating. Brooke's decision to switch to a thicker iron had been justified.

From the fall of 1861 until February 1862 the Tredegar foundry worked almost continuously on the armor plating for the *Merrimac*. One of the owners remarked that "we are pressed almost beyond endurance," but they nonetheless continued their tireless production. By mid-October almost one hundred tons of plating had been rolled, but it sat on the banks of the James River for want of flatcars and engines to deliver it to Norfolk. The Confederate Army Quartermaster Bureau, which was responsible for all rail shipments, faced a growing logistical problem because of a shortage of engines, cars, and rail time. The *Merrimac*'s iron plating had to be transported to Weldon, North Carolina, before it could finally be loaded aboard a less-traveled rail line for transportation to Norfolk. Although Tredegar officials had estimated that the iron would all be delivered to navy yard by the end of November, the last shipment did not arrive until February 12, 1862.

By the time Jones arrived at Norfolk the *Merrimac* was far behind schedule for completion. Nonetheless, Jones began

searching for a crew and officers for his unfinished vessel.
Finding officers presented no problem since many qualified
candidates had seceded. In January 1862 the Navy
Department instructed Lieutenant John Taylor Wood to report
to Norfolk, and Jones entrusted Wood with finding the necessary three hundred seamen. In fact, recruiting them proved dif-
ficult because the South lacked an established maritime cul-
ture. Jones and Wood ultimately had to travel to Yorktown,
Richmond, and Petersburg to find soldiers with sea legs. As
late as February 10, 1862, the *Merrimac* still had not received
its full crew complement.

At the beginning of 1862 the ship's stern remained unar-
mored. Meanwhile, Jones found increasing difficulty as he
tried to train his crew for service on an ironclad, without an
ironclad to train aboard. By mid-January, in an effort to expedite the ship's completion, machinists, blacksmiths, and bolt
drivers agreed to work until 8 P.M. seven days a week until
they had finished the project. Even so, work proceeded slowly
and delays seemed to be the rule rather than the exception.
While the ship was completely armored by January 27, Jones's
frustration became apparent when he remarked that "some-
body ought to be hung."

On February 17, 1862, the *Merrimac*, rechristened the
C.S.S. *Virginia* even though virtually all referred to her by her
former name, slid out of the dry dock into the murky waters of
the Elizabeth River. It was an unceremonious event witnessed
by few: crew member William R. Cline remarked that "there
were no invitations to governors and other distinguished men,
no sponsor nor maid, no bottle of wine, no brass band, no
blowing of steam whistles, no great crowds to witness this
memorable event." One or two officers observed this mile-
stone, and only five men stood aboard the vessel when she slid
into the water.

Three days after her launching Jones complained that
"there has not been a dry spot aboard of her, leaks every-

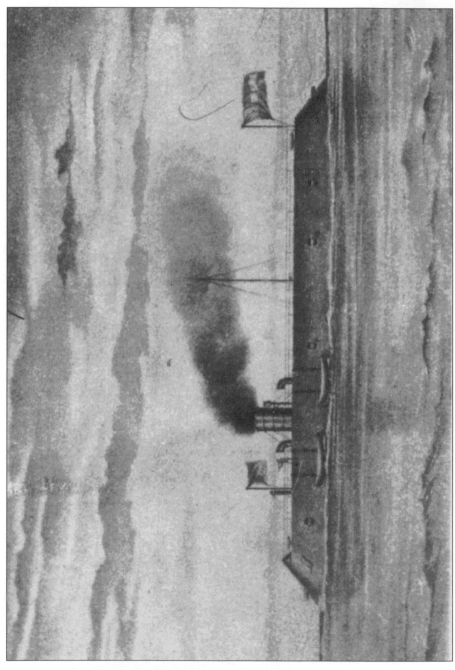

Ther *Merrimac*, rechristened the C.S.S. *Virginia*

where." Apparently the extensive caulking along the seams had been inadequate. Moreover, the ship was badly ventilated, uncomfortable, and very unhealthy. The conditions resulted in sickness to one-third of the crew and gave everyone reason for complaint. Throughout the end of February, Jones tried to drill and train his crew in the necessary practices aboard the vessel while officers and marines reported for duty. Until the eve of the attack in Hampton Roads mechanics scurried around frantically trying to finish repairs on the ironclad warrior.

The Confederate ship was an untried novelty. Even so, she appeared to many to be a formidable antagonist. With a hull measuring almost 263 feet from bow to stern, she had a 178 ft. 3 in. iron casemated base atop her hull sloping upward at a thirty-six degree angle. The casemated sides, twenty-four feet from waterline to top, consisted of an outer shell of two two-inch layers of iron plate fastened horizontally by metal bolts to a two feet solid pine and four-inch oak backing. Porter had placed four gun ports on each side of the casemate, and three seven-inch rifle ports at each end. The main deck, also covered with iron plating, stretched 29 ft. 6 in. in front of the casemate and 55 feet to the rear. Just below the waterline on the bow, Secretary Mallory had insisted that Porter install a fifteen-hundred-pound cast-iron ram.

Although the *Merrimac* was a fearsome weapon, she had many flaws. Since Porter had expressed misgivings about attaching a ram to the bow, he did a lackadaisical job of installing it. In fact, one of the flanges mounting the ram cracked during assembly and was never repaired. More importantly, according to Jones, Porter had miscalculated the ship's weight. The result was that the *Merrimac* sat too high in the water, leaving her virtually unprotected hull exposed. To remedy this flaw pig-iron ballast, in addition to the supplies, powder, shells, and 150 tons of coal needed for operation, had to be added to correct the ship's displacement. But even after everything had been loaded the ironclad still sat too high as the casemate extended only six inches below the waterline. Furthermore, no extra ballast could be added for fear of straining the ship's bottom; should an enemy gunner fire a true shot it could be fatal to the long-awaited Confederate ship.

By late February 1862 the renovated *Merrimac* was being repaired and loaded with supplies and equipment. Her crew and officers were reporting for duty with the exception of her captain. Catesby ap Roger Jones had hoped that he would be given command of the former burned and blackened hulk. Yet the navy's system of seniority sunk any possibility of him commanding the newly commissioned ironclad. "Jones is not old enough" wrote Lieutenant John Taylor Wood; other more senior officers had appealed to Secretary Mallory for command of the vessel. Mallory named sixty-one-year-old Captain Franklin Buchanan, who had visited the ironclad only once

Franklin Buchanan: Born Maryland 1800; Buchanan entered the U.S. Navy in 1815 as a midshipman and after several years at sea was promoted to lieutenant in 1825; promoted to commander in 1841, he assisted Secretary of the Navy George Bancroft in the founding of the U.S. Naval Academy and in 1845 became its first superintendent; two years later, he left the academy to command the sloop *Germantown* during the Mexican War; he commanded Matthew C. Perry's flagship *Susquehanna* during the expedition to Japan that opened that nation to U.S. trade and diplomatic relations; in 1855 he was promoted to captain and given command of the Washington Navy Yard; in 1861, after Massachusetts troops were fired upon in Baltimore, Buchanan assumed that Maryland would secede and tendered his resignation; when Maryland failed to secede, he attempted to withdraw his resignation but his request was denied; in August 1861 he offered his services to the Confederacy and was appointed a captain in the Confederate Navy the following month; after heading the Office of Orders and Details, Buchanan became in February 1862 flag officer in command

during her stay in dry dock, as flag officer in command of the naval defenses on the James River. The captain had been instructed to use the *Merrimac* as the flagship of his station and, if possible, ascend the Potomac River as far as Washington, D.C.

From the beginning of the war the basic Union strategy had followed General Winfield Scott's "Anaconda Plan," which called for blockading all Southern ports on the Atlantic and Gulf coasts, while simultaneously augmenting the army. Once the regular army had been increased and trained, it would be used in conjunction with navy gunboats to divide the Confederacy along its major waterways; the South would then be divided, completely surrounded, and isolated from outside help. Afterward, the Union noose would be slowly tightened around the Confederate neck until the South withered from the war.

of the James River defenses and the Chesapeake Bay Squadron; his flagship became the newly completed ironclad *Virginia* (*Merrimac*), with which he attacked the Federal blockading fleet in Hampton Roads on 8 March 1862; after sinking the U.S.S. *Cumberland* and bombarding the U.S.S. *Congress* into submission, fire from Federal forces ashore interrupted the surrender process and Buchanan ordered the frigate destroyed; Buchanan took up a rifle to participate in the destruction but a Federal rifle ball struck the captain's leg and disabled him; Lieutenant Catesby ap Roger Jones commanded the *Virginia* (*Merrimac*) the following day in its famous battle with the Federal ironclad *Monitor*; promoted to full admiral in August 1862, Buchanan became the highest ranking officer in the Confederate States Navy; in September he assumed command of Mobile's defenses and worked diligently to improve the situation there; during Federal Admiral David G. Farragut's 5 August 1864 attack on Mobile, most of Buchanan's fleet was quickly destroyed, leaving only his flagship, the recently completed ironclad *Tennessee* to face Farragut's entire fleet; after a spirited battle, in which Buchanan was again wounded, the *Tennessee* was surrounded and compelled to surrender; captured and imprisoned, Buchanan was not exchanged until March 1865; again assigned to Mobile, he did not reach the city before its fall to Federal forces in April; he surrendered in May; after the war he served briefly as president of Maryland Agricultural College and worked for a time as an insurance executive; Admiral Buchanan died at his Maryland home in 1874.

Mallory believed the *Merrimac* and other ironclads could break the Union blockade and prevent Confederate defeat. And should she wreak destruction on a Federal squadron in the Chesapeake Bay in her first test, Mallory anticipated that the *Merrimac* could "eclipse all the glories of the combats of the sea." She could destroy Washington, D.C., the city's navy yard, and all the bridges spanning the Potomac. Moreover, should calm seas prevail, the ironclad could steam north to New York City, where Mallory believed that a successful attack "by a single ship, would do more to achieve our immediate independence than would the results of many campaigns." According to Mallory, such a demonstration would not only have military significance, but diplomatic importance as well; it might persuade England and/or France to formally recognize the South and provide military support, without which the Confederacy could not expect to fight a prolonged war. Thus, when the *Merrimac* finally steamed into the Chesapeake, she would be encountering more than just the Federal blockading fleet, the ironclad would be fighting for the very survival of the Confederacy.

Saturday morning, March 8, 1862, began as a clear spring day with bright skies and calm waters off Norfolk. Within this tranquility there was increasing hustle and bustle at the Gosport Navy Yard, just as there had been for the past several weeks. But this day would be different because Captain Buchanan was going to take the *Merrimac* down river on what most believed would be a trial run. Buchanan, however, had different intentions.

3
"A TIN CAN ON A SHINGLE"

During the late summer and early fall of 1861, while Southern carpenters in Norfolk cleared away the charred timbers of the *Merrimac* and rebuilt her upper decks, engineers, entrepreneurs, and inventors descended on Washington, D.C. to present ship plans to the U.S. Navy's Ironclad Board. Among the would-be ironclad builders was the cantankerous Swedish-born engineer John Ericsson, whose path had already been smoothed by an influential contact, the Connecticut entrepreneur Cornelius Scranton Bushnell.

Secretary of the Navy Gideon Welles, a levelheaded and efficient administrator, had been slow to grasp the importance or necessity of an ironclad fleet, even though he had heard information and rumors about Confederate plans for the *Merrimac*. Although inexperienced in technical matters, Welles nonetheless immersed himself in the subject by conferring with his naval advisors and assistant secretary. By early August, he had convinced himself and President Abraham Lincoln of the necessity of an iron fleet to oppose Confederate ironclads under construction. He asked Congress for an appropriation, he appointed a three-member examining board to study proposals and make recommendations, and he issued an advertisement soliciting designs for the experimental iron vessel. Within days, seventeen proposals had been submitted and the board began reviewing the projects and interviewing the applicants; the board ultimately narrowed the list to two candidates—C.S. Bushnell and Company of New Haven, Connecticut and Merrick and Sons of Philadelphia.

In mid-August, Bushnell appeared before the board to answer queries about his project. During the meeting, however, the officers asked several technical questions about the novel design of Bushnell's ship, the *Galena*, which the New

John Ericsson: Born Sweden 1903; Ericsson evidenced his talents for mechanical engineering at an early age and worked on numerous projects in his native Sweden; at seventeen he was commissioned into the Swedish army and was quickly promoted to lieutenant; he developed plans for improved canal systems and invented a caloric engine; in 1826 he secured a leave to promote his engine in England, an effort that went unrewarded; although promoted to captain, he never returned to duty and obtained a discharge in 1827; remaining in England, he produced several important inventions, largely for maritime application; in 1828 he produced an experimental steamship, followed in 1829 by his steam carriage *Novelty*, that competed unsuccessfully with George Stephenson's *Rocket*, and a steam fire engine; he continued to work with steam technology and locomotive engineering, and in 1833 produced an improved caloric engine; in 1836 he patented a screw propeller and the following year produced a twin-screw steamship; in 1839 Ericsson left England for the United States; shortly thereafter, he designed for the U.S. Navy the *Princeton*, the first screw-propelled steam warship

Englander could not answer. Some hours later Cornelius H. Delamater of New York, an engineering acquaintance who was also on business in Washington, suggested that Bushnell travel to New York City to discuss the board's concerns with the distinguished inventor and engineer John Ericsson. That evening Bushnell traveled by train to New York and the following morning he met with Ericsson.

Bushnell presented Ericsson with pertinent information concerning the *Galena* as well as the questions of the Ironclad Board. The engineer made some hasty calculations, and told Bushnell that the *Galena's* design was sound and could withstand six-inch solid shot. This assurance pleased Bushnell greatly. But Ericsson also asked if the entrepreneur would be interested in examining a ship design that could defy the heaviest shot or shell. Of course Bushnell was interested. Ericsson

with all machinery and boilers below the water line; this revolutionary vessel contained dozens of inventions that made it the prototype for a new generation of warships; during a demonstration in 1844, *Princeton's* twelve-inch gun exploded, killing several witnesses, including the secretaries of state and the navy; although Ericsson had not designed the gun he attracted much of the blame and fell out of government favor; Ericsson, who became a U.S. citizen in 1848, remained a prolific designer but his attempts to sell an ironclad warship proved unavailing; in 1854 he submitted to Emperor Napoleon III a plan for an armored warship with a revolving gun turret, but was again disappointed; finally, with the coming of the Civil War, Ericsson received in 1861 a contract from the U.S. government to produce an ironclad warship; the steam *Monitor*, completed in February 1862, featured a heavily armored revolving two-gun turret on a flat deck just above the water line with machinery, magazines, quarters, and stores well below the water line; the battle between the *Monitor* and the C.S.S. *Virginia* (*Merrimac*) in March 1862 revolutionized naval warfare and signaled the end for wooden warships; under Ericsson's direction, dozens of similar vessels were built for the U.S. Navy during the war; Ericsson-inspired or -designed ironclads soon appeared in navies around the world; in the 1870s he designed the *Destroyer*, a vessel that again changed naval warfare with its ability to fire subsurface torpedoes; Ericsson remained active in the evolution of naval technology and worked extensively with solar energy until his death at New York in 1889.

Gideon Welles: born Connecticut 1802; he attended the Episcopal Academy at Cheshire, Connecticut, and the American Literary, Scientific, and Military Academy at Norwich, Vermont; he also studied law, but embarked on a career in journalism; in 1826 he became an owner and the editor of the *Hartford Times*; that year he won election to the Connecticut legislature, where he served until 1835; he fought against debt-related imprisonment, religious- and property-based voting requirements, and authored the state's first general incorporation laws; he supported individual freedom, strict construction of the Constitution, and states' rights; elected three times to the state office of comptroller of public accounts, he was appointed postmaster of Hartford 1836; in 1846 he began a four-year stint as chief of the

Navy's Bureau of Provisions and Clothing; in 1850 he failed to win election to the U.S. Senate; a long-time Democrat he joined the Republicans, chiefly over the slavery issue; in 1856 he helped establish the pro-Republican *Hartford Evening Press*, and became a frequent contributor; also that year he lost a bid to become governor of Connecticut; in 1860 president-elect Abraham Lincoln selected Welles for his cabinet; in March 1861 he became secretary of the Navy and took on the daunting job of building and modernizing a naval force during a time of war; in this he was quite successful; he oversaw massive ship-building projects, the development of ironclad vessels, and important advances in armaments and ordnance; his was among the government's most efficiently run departments; he was also a strong moderating influence within Lincoln's cabinet; although fiercely loyal to the president, he opposed Lincoln's excessive uses of power, such as the suppression of the press and the suspension of *Habeas Corpus*; he vigorously supported Lincoln's moderate approach to restoring Southern states to the Union and, after Lincoln's assassination, provided the same support for President Andrew Johnson, steadfastly backing him during the impeachment proceedings; after his retirement in 1869, Welles wrote several articles and published a book, *Lincoln and Seward*, in 1874; Welles died in 1878; he was one of only two cabinet members to serve throughout Lincoln's administration; the *Diary of Gideon Welles*, published posthumously in three volumes, remains among the most important historical sources from that period.

scurried away and quickly returned with a small, dust-covered box which contained a model and plans for his own ironclad ship. The inventor then explained the ship's most impressive features: the power it could project and the punishment it could withstand; inexpensive construction cost; and the speed with which she could be built. After examining the model and designs, Bushnell asked Ericsson if he could present them to his friend, Secretary of the Navy Gideon Welles. Ericsson agreed and the entrepreneur left at once for Hartford, Connecticut.

When Bushnell showed the plans to Welles, the secretary "was favorably impressed." He asked the entrepreneur to present them to the Ironclad Board immediately. Bushnell hurried back to the capital where he met with President Abraham Lincoln on September 12. The president apparently was also "greatly pleased" by the design and even agreed to go with Bushnell to the board the following day. Shortly after noon on 13 September, the board, having heard all of Bushnell's pleas and arguments, rejected the project. Refusing to quit, Bushnell traveled to New York where he told the Swedish engineer, not that his design had been refused, but that the board wanted more information. Ericsson packed his bags and departed for Washington, arriving early on the morning of September 15, 1861.

Bushnell's ruse began to unravel when the Ironclad Board reluctantly agreed to meet with Ericsson. The officers, as a matter of formality, posed a series of questions which the inventor huffily answered. As Ericsson prepared to leave, the officers informed him that his proposal had already been rejected because it did not demonstrate sufficient stability. This was the chance Bushnell had hoped for, because it allowed the engineer the opportunity to articulate the finer points of his ironclad's design. With unusual modesty and patience, Ericsson reiterated much of the explanations he had given Bushnell a month earlier. According to Bushnell the eloquent description of the ship's merits began to sway all in the room. When Ericsson finished, the board members retired to a corner before asking if he would return at one o'clock 1 P.M. to present his arguments again.

Later that afternoon Ericsson again persuasively articulated his case before the board and now Secretary Welles as well. Yet again the inventor was asked to return at a later hour. At three o'clock an exhausted Ericsson reappeared at the Navy Department, prepared again to argue his case. Yet when he arrived he was escorted into Welles's office and informed that his presentation had convinced the board; Ericsson would receive a contract to begin building his ironclad warship at once. The Navy Department was finally giving John Ericsson a chance—one that had been a long time in coming.

Ericsson was born in 1803 in the central Sweden mining village of Langbanshyttan. As a young boy he had worked for his father as a cartographer and by age thirteen had become so proficient that his father allowed him to lead a surveying crew. Less than four years later, he joined the Engineering Corps of the Swedish Army and soon found himself designing and building steam engines for mining use. By age twenty-three Ericsson's work had taken him to London where he built a steam fire engine; fire and insurance companies, however, rejected the machine because it took too long to put into operation and used too much water. He also designed a marine steam engine for Arctic exploration that owner John Ross placed in too large a vessel; when the ship became icebound Ross blamed Ericsson for the failure. In August 1829 Ericsson's tiny steam locomotive *Novelty* outperformed George and Robert Stephenson's *Rocket*, but it did not win the Liverpool & Manchester Railway's prize for the competition; judges chose to disqualify Ericsson's locomotive because of a tiny leak in the *Novelty*'s boiler even though it had won the contest. The inventor later designed a new screw propeller and installed it on the steam tug *The Flying Devil*; for no apparent reason the Lords of the Admiralty refused to consider such a vessel for the Royal Navy. Ericsson seemed to encounter nothing but obstacles, and as a result in 1839 he left England for the United States.

American naval officer Robert Stockton had heard of Ericsson's screw propeller steam tug and after observing it thought that such a vessel could benefit the U.S. Navy. In fact, Stockton persuaded Ericsson to move to New York so that he could oversee construction of a propeller-driven warship. The vessel, later named the *Princeton*, became the world's most advanced naval craft as she was the first metal-hull, screw-propelled steam warship. She also proved to be one of the fastest ships in the world. More memorable, however, was the unfortunate explosion of the *Princeton*'s large gun, "Peacemaker," on February 28, 1844, which killed Secretary of State Abel P. Upshur and Secretary of the Navy Thomas W. Gilmer as well as several other dignitaries. Stockton blamed Ericsson for the explosion and afterward the Navy Department refused to consider any of the inventor's proposals.

Residing in New York City, Ericsson continued designing steam engines and screw propellers. In the early 1850s he built the caloric-powered (hot-air engine), side-wheel ship *Ericsson* which later sank in rough weather when someone forgot to close her ports. Although the disaster was not directly his fault, the inventor was greatly embarrassed and considered it the only failure of his career. But even this blemish did not discourage Ericsson. In September 1854 he sent a model and plans of a steam-powered ironclad with a revolving one-gun turret to Napoleon III, whose nation was involved in the Crimean War. The conflict ended just as Ericsson's material arrived and the French emperor returned it in a small box, with a note of thanks. Ericsson kept the box in his closet and forgot about it until September 1861 when Bushnell visited.

On October 25, 1861, a little more than a month after Ericsson and Bushnell first met, workers laid the wooden keel for an ironclad warship at the Continental Iron Works in Greenpoint, Long Island, New York. That same late October day the Swedish inventor also signed with his subcontractors. The Rensselaer Works would provide the bar iron and rivets for the main deck; the Albany Iron Works, New York's Holdane & Company, and H. Abbot & Company in Baltimore would roll the armor plating; other companies from Buffalo, and Nashua, New Hampshire would fashion vital special parts. Ericsson's intricate designs allowed him to save valuable time through simultaneous manufacturing. It also allowed him to bring the parts together for rapid assembly with little if any alteration.

The novel warship began to take shape under Ericsson's careful eye during the fall of 1861. Carpenters worked around the clock to complete the hull and prepare it for an iron sheathing, and the various parts arrived in the foundry yard

John Lorimer Worden: Born New York 1818; Worden entered the U.S. Navy as a midshipman in 1835 and, after attending the Philadelphia Naval School, in 1840

became a passed midshipman; promoted to lieutenant in 1846, he served at sea for several years and at the Naval Observatory; at the outbreak of the Civil War Worden was dispatched to Fort Pickens, Florida, with orders for the Federal garrison there to hold out; in April 1861, while attempting an overland return to Washington, Worden was seized as a prisoner of war and held until October; selected to command the experimental ironclad *Monitor* then under construction in New York, Worden supervised the vessel's completion and led it southward to defend the Federal blockading fleet in Hampton Roads from the Confederate ironclad ram *Virginia*; after a harrowing voyage, during which the *Monitor* almost foundered, the revolutionary warship arrived at Hampton Roads late on 8 March 1862, too late to save the *Congress* and *Cumberland* from destruction by the new Rebel menace; the following morning Worden moved out to protect the remaining

and were assembled to the ship. She was a small vessel by the standards of the day—only 172 feet from bow to stern and 41 feet wide. Her flat deck, composed of solid wood covered with one-inch iron plating, extended only eighteen inches above the waterline. At the center of the deck stood the twenty-feet-wide, nine-feet-high gun turret, housing two eleven-inch Dahlgren guns and encased in eight inches of iron plating. Other than the turret, only a 3 ft. 10 in. pilothouse rose above the deck. The vessel displaced about 1,000 tons, which meant that she drew only 10 ft. 6 in. of water, a draft that would allow her to operate in virtually any harbor. It was a curious design that resembled, as one observer remarked, "a tin can on a shingle."

Ericsson had promised the Navy Department that the ship would be ready for service by January 12, 1862. But by early January skeptics were beginning to bemoan the ironclad nov-

Federal ships and thus initiated the famous duel between the *Monitor* and the *Virginia* (*Merrimac*); he boldly captained the *Monitor* in the intense battle until a shell explosion near the slit in the pilot house through which he was viewing the action rendered him blind and disabled from further action; Lieutenant Samuel Dana Greene assumed command but could not pursue the withdrawing *Virginia*; the *Monitor* succeeded in saving the wooden fleet and dispelling fears that the Confederate ironclad would capture Washington or even New York; for this, Worden and his crew received the Thanks of Congress; after sixteen years as a lieutenant, Warden was promoted to commander in July 1862 and to captain in February 1863; recovering from his injuries, Worden commanded the monitor *Montauk* in the South Atlantic Blockading Squadron; the *Montauk* destroyed the Confederate commerce raider *Nashville* on the Ogeechee River in Georgia, and participated in Admiral S.F. DuPont's unsuccessful attack on Charleston in April 1863; thereafter Worden was ordered to New York, where he spent the balance of the war in the development of improved ironclad warships; after the war he commanded the *Pensacola* in the Pacific Squadron and was promoted to commodore in 1868; he served as superintendent of the Naval Academy from 1870 to 1874, during which time he was elevated to rear admiral; he commaded the European Squadron from 1875 to 1877 and thereafter served on the Examining and Retiring Boards until his retirement in 1886— completing a fifty-year navy career; Admiral Worden died at New York in 1897.

elty as yet another "Ericsson's folly." Secretary Welles maintained faith in the project and with the assistance of Commodore Joseph Smith, Sr., began to consider commanders for the vessel. After much discussion and study Smith recommended a New Yorker, Lieutenant John Lorimer Worden, as he believed the officer possessed the necessary qualities for this precarious experimental command. Smith wrote to the junior lieutenant, "you are the right sort of officer to put in command of her."

Worden, who had entered the Navy as a midshipman in 1834, spent three years in the South Atlantic Squadron and seven months at the Philadelphia Naval School before the department promoted him to passed midshipman in July 1840. During the early 1840s, he served under Thomas ap Catesby Jones in the Pacific Squadron when that officer in October 1842 captured Monterey, California; the United States and Mexico, however, were not at war. During and after the Mexican War, Worden was again with the Pacific Squadron aboard the store ship Southampton and other vessels. In the 1850s the lieutenant served with the Mediterranean and Home squadrons before taking a post at the United States Naval Observatory at Washington, D.C. With the outbreak of the Civil War the Navy Department sent Worden south from Washington on a secret mission to deliver orders to naval forces at Pensacola, Florida. After successfully completing his assignment, Worden attempted to return north overland but he was captured near Montgomery, Alabama, and remained a prisoner for seven months. In fact, he was still suffering from illness and complications due to his confinement as late as his appointment as commander of the Union ironclad.

On January 16, 1862, four days after the scheduled completion date, Worden reported for duty aboard the unfinished ship. While the work of completing the vessel continued, the lieutenant aggressively recruited the necessary men for his crew. From the North Carolina and Sabine, ships used for receiving recruits, the officer enlisted the fifty-seven men he estimated were needed for the ironclad. Twenty-one-year-old Lieutenant Samuel Dana Greene of Maryland joined as the executive officer and eight other junior officers, not including the civilian Acting Assistant Paymaster William F. Keeler, also signed aboard the ship. Keeler, who gained his appointment through an influential Illinois congressman, had never served in the Navy, and did not even own a uniform. He later learned, to his surprise, that he would not be allowed to go to sea without a uniform and had to purchase a new suit of blues.

Throughout the last half of January Worden's men brought

Samuel Dana Greene: Born Maryland 1839; Greene was graduated from the U.S. Naval Academy in 1859; commissioned a midshipman, he served aboard the *Hartford* in the China Squadron before returning to the United States at the outbreak of the Civil War; promoted to lieutenant in 1861, he volunteered for service on the ironclad *Monitor*; as executive officer of the *Monitor* during its battle with the C.S.S. *Virginia* (*Merrimac*) in March 1862, Greene directed the ships guns until forced to assume command on the wounding of Lieutenant John L. Worden; Greene continued in command until the appointment of Commander John P. Bankhead; he resumed the position of executive officer and was on duty when the *Monitor* foundered and sank off Cape Hatteras, North Carolina, in December 1862; thereafter he served aboard the *Florida* in the South Atlantic Blockading Squadron in 1863 and on the *Iroquois* in the pursuit of Confederate commerce raiders in 1864 and 1865; promoted to lieutenant commander in 1865 and to commander in 1872, he held numerous ship commands and taught mathematics and astronomy at the Naval Academy; Commander Greene committed suicide while serving as executive officer at the Portsmouth Navy Yard in 1884. His father, George Sears Greene, was a noted engineer and general in the Federal army during the Civil War.

Officers aboard the *Monitor*, July 9, 1862; back row left to right: George Frederickson, Mark Sunstrom, Paymaster William Keeler, Isaac Newton; middle row: Lieutenant Samuel D. Greene, Master Louis N. Stodder, Edwin V. Gager, William Flye, Surgeon Daniel C. Logue; bottom row: Robinson Hands and Albert Campbell.

aboard their personal effects and tried to become accustomed to their new iron home. The officers had comfortable private quarters as Ericsson had spared no expense on their cabins. Each of them had a bed set into the wall, closets for clothing, and shelves for books, a washbasin, and storage. Keeler remarked that he had seen accommodations aboard several vessels, but had "seen no room as handsomely fitted up as ours." On the other hand, however, the seamen slept in hammocks in a common open space aft of the officers' cabins. Their accommodations were poorly ventilated, cold, and uncomfortable, and apart from nearby storage lockers offered virtually no privacy for personal possessions. One could hardly forget that this vessel was designed for war and not comfort.

As the time for launching quickly approached, Secretary Welles wrote Ericsson asking if the inventor would like to suggest a name for the ship. After careful consideration, the inventor wrote that "the iron-clad intruder will thus prove a severe monitor" (that is, the deliverer of a severe warning) to Confederate leaders. He also remarked that even England would look with interest on "this last 'Yankee notion,' this monitor." Thus, "I propose to name the new battery *Monitor*." Ten days later, on January 30, 1862, the *Monitor* unceremoniously slid out of her dock at Greenpoint into the East River and floated just as the inventor had promised. The following day Worden fired up the ironclad's boilers and made steam for the first time.

Although the *Monitor* was ready for sea, she still awaited the two Dahlgren guns for her turret. Worden had already appealed to the commandant of the Brooklyn Navy Yard for twelve-inch Dahlgren smoothbore cannon, but the commander had none available. In fact, the eleven-inch cannon Worden ultimately secured had to be removed from the docked ship *Dacotah*. In any case, by February 15 the guns had been installed and sighted in, and last-minute preparations were being completed. Four days later Ericsson turned the ship over to Worden, and at 2 P.M. on February 19 the *Monitor* moved from her moorings at Greenpoint towards the Brooklyn Navy Yard. The ironclad's first official voyage was inauspicious as she experienced engine and boiler problems and had to be towed into wharf at 7:30 P.M. Repairs were quickly completed and the *Monitor* was commissioned as a fourth-rate warship in the United States Navy on February 25, 1862.

The *Monitor* was scheduled to steam south to the Chesapeake Bay the day following her commissioning, but the loading of coal, ammunition, and supplies delayed her departure until February 27. Snow fell that early morning as the *Monitor* steamed towards the Manhattan side of the East River. But as she made her way, the helmsman found that he could not control her rudder. The ironclad "ran first to the New York side then to the Brooklyn & so back & forth across the river, first to one side then to the other, like a drunken man on a side walk." At last the *Monitor* crashed into the New York gas works, and Worden had the ship towed back into harbor.

The commander at the Brooklyn yard suggested that a new rudder be installed. But Ericsson exploded at such a proposition, "The *Monitor* is mine, and I say it shall not be done." He insisted that such an alteration would take the Navy a month to complete, whereas he could take care of the problem in only three days; and so he did, by adjusting the steering apparatus and correcting the problem with the rudder. On March 3, when Worden again put the *Monitor* to sea, the ironclad was accompanied by a three-man navy commission. This time rain saturated the trial, but apart from the resulting slippery deck, all went as well as Ericsson, Worden, or anyone could have expected. Although the *Monitor* passed her test, inclement weather prevented her departure until 4 P.M. on March 6, 1862.

When the *Monitor* pulled away from the Brooklyn Navy Yard for the Atlantic, accompanied by the steamers *Sachem* and *Currituck* and the steam tug *Seth Low*, crowds of people lined the bank to cheer her departure. Although few of the sailors or officers aboard the ironclad knew exactly where her destination lay, they all had their suspicions. Worden, however, had been ordered by Welles to "proceed with the U.S.S. *Monitor*.... to Hampton Roads, Virginia" to keep the Confederate ironclad, then nearing completion, confined to the Chesapeake Bay. If the Union vessel did not succeed, some believed that the Confederate ship "will be almost certain to commit great depredations on our armed and unarmed vessels in Hampton Roads." An even greater fear was that perhaps the *Merrimac* would move on Washington, D.C. and hold the capital under siege.

On the trip south along the Jersey coast the officers experienced the common problems associated with developing a shipboard routine. The seamen would arise at five o'clock and have their morning meal while the officers generally slept until eight o'clock. After eating, all began their assigned tasks at which they were occupied throughout the day. After dinner the men would have a few moments of free time before they bedded down for the evening. Over a prolonged period of close confinement, tension and anxiety wore away at civility, leaving all on edge. After spending a few days aboard the ironclad, Keeler bluntly informed his wife that "some of the officers as I get better acquainted with them I like better, others not so well." No one knew exactly what to expect as they steamed for their unknown destination.

The trip initially provided no surprises as the *Monitor* and her escorts easily traversed the calm seas. In fact, the night of March 6 began with little excitement. But by morning the seas had begun to swell as a westerly gale overtook the tiny ironclad. The waves grew higher and higher, washing over the deck and unexpectedly into the hold. Before the *Monitor* had sailed, the gun turret had been elevated and a hemp rope inserted between its brass ball bearings and its casing, in the hope that this would provide an effective watertight seal. It did not. On

the morning of March 7 water poured into the ship as witnesses observed, "like a waterfall" leaving it "wet & very disagree-
able." By noon the winds had increased and waves poured over
the six-foot-high smoke stack that had been attached for the
voyage. Water began to permeate every seal within the ship
and all began to worry.

The water that oozed in began to take its toll further below.
The drive belts of the air blowers became soaked and slipped
so that they could not turn the fans. Without air circulation,
carbon dioxide from the fires heating the boilers filled the
engine room. Within minutes four apparently dead bodies were
brought topside and the gas began to move from the engine
room to adjacent chambers. Lieutenant Greene and Paymaster
Keeler both went below to help others escape death by suffo-
cation, and both barely survived themselves. Shortly after four
o'clock the water smothered the boiler fires, the engines as
well as the air fans and water pumps quit, and the *Monitor* lay
helpless. With men crowded aboard her slippery deck,
Lieutenant Greene signaled the *Seth Low* and had her tow the
ironclad near shore where the waters were calmer. By eight
o'clock that evening the deadly gases below had cleared and
engineers could begin repairing the vessel.

During the night another similar problem emerged as water
again flooded through the *Monitor's* anchor well. All expected
a replay of that horrible afternoon. Lieutenant Greene began
"to think that the *Monitor* would never see daylight."
Fortunately by three o'clock the following morning the seas
had calmed; the *Seth Low* continued to tow the ironclad south.
At noon the Union convoy passed Cape Charles, the southern
tip of Maryland, entered Chesapeake Bay, and within an hour
was but fifteen miles off Fort Monroe and Hampton Roads,
their ultimate destination.

As the *Monitor* steamed to the west those aboard heard
heavy cannon fire and saw clouds of smoke in the distance.
With darkness approaching, the men aboard the ironclad

observed that "the flashes of guns lit up the distant horizon & bursting shells flashed in the air." The sailors could only guess what was happening off Fort Monroe, but many believed correctly that the Confederate ironclad had introduced herself to the Union Navy. About ten miles from the fort the *Monitor* took aboard the harbor pilot who would guide the ironclad through the shoals. He confirmed to the officers who surrounded him on deck that the *Merrimac* had finally come down the Elizabeth River. Moreover, she was demolishing the Union fleet off Hampton Roads. Many wondered how one ship could wreak such havoc on an entire squadron. But as they neared the fort their questions were answered by the red and yellow glowing hulk of a United States frigate of war engulfed by flames. Tomorrow, March 9, 1862, the *Monitor* would have its chance to stop the Confederate leviathan.

4
"AN ORDINARY TRIAL TRIP"

Since mid-February 1862 Franklin Buchanan had been preparing the *Merrimac* for action. The Confederate Navy Department had procured the oil necessary for the ship's heavy machinery, and secured nearly 18,000 pounds of powder to fill the vessel's magazines. Catesby Jones had enlisted a crew, and officers had signed aboard the experimental craft. By Friday, March 7, the ship was ready for its first test.

During late February and early March, as the ironclad was being readied, Buchanan had been planning his course of action. Originally, he had wanted a joint army-navy attack against Federal forces at Hampton Roads and Newport News, Virginia. But heavy winter rains had left roads virtually impassable for both Confederate artillery and infantry. His second choice was to proceed quietly at night down the Elizabeth River and, at dawn, attack and destroy the Federal fleet and shore batteries at Newport News. Although this was

Buchanan's only practical option, this strategy also encountered unforeseen obstacles.

The same storm front that almost sunk the *Monitor* in the Atlantic wreaked havoc on Buchanan's preparations at Norfolk. Inclement weather forced him to wait. Moreover, on the evening of March 7, Buchanan learned that his river pilots refused to guide an untested ship at night through a rough river not marked with buoys, and especially not at night and without running lights. Buchanan could only hope that daybreak would bring clear skies and calm waters. But as he waited, Buchanan pondered a dispatch that had arrived earlier that morning from Secretary of the Navy Stephen Mallory. The secretary suggested that Buchanan proceed against Federal forces at Hampton Roads before making a bold strike against Washington, D.C., New York, or Boston. If Buchanan would comply with this suggestion, Mallory contended that "peace would inevitably follow." Buchanan's vision, however, was more realistic. He could consider no further plans until the Yankee fleet at Hampton Roads had been eliminated.

The morning of Saturday, March 8, 1862, brought the clear skies for which Buchanan had hoped. Mechanics finished their check of the ship's machinery while workmen hastily spread a thick coat of grease to the ironclad's casemated sides. Confederates believed this lubricant would increase the possibility that missiles would glance off the vessel. At last, the *Merrimac* stood ready for her supposed shakedown cruise; only Buchanan, Jones, Secretary Mallory, Major General John B. Magruder, commanding a small Confederate force at Yorktown, and John R. Tucker, commanding three small Confederate vessels in the James River, knew the ironclad's true destination. Lieutenant John R. Eggleston recalled that "we thought we were going on an ordinary trial trip." This was, after all, the ship's first time out. Many others, however, including Lieutenant John Taylor Wood, believed that they were going to experience more than a trial. In fact, shortly before the ironclad departed, a group of lieutenants attended a church service and even took the Holy Sacrament of the Lord's Supper for the first time since they arrived at Norfolk.

Private James Keenan of the 2d Georgia Infantry Battalion, stationed in Norfolk, remembered that "at 11:00 a gun was fired at the Navy Yard, which appeared to be the signal for something." Events happened quickly thereafter and before the smoke from the signal gun had cleared, Buchanan had ordered his flag officer's red ensign hoisted, and the ship's docking lines had been cast off. The *Merrimac* slowly moved into the Elizabeth River, as the last of the mechanics jumped onto the pier. Surprisingly, the ironclad's twenty-two foot draft barely permitted her to float in the river's half-flood tide; fortunately for Buchanan the water continued to rise throughout the afternoon. Along both sides of the river people crowded to witness the spectacle, to wave handkerchiefs in support, and to honor the significance of the moment. Keenan remarked that "in an instant the whole city was in an uproar, women, children, men on horseback and on foot running down towards the river from every conceivable direction shouting, 'the *Merrimac* is going down.'" Although Midshipman Hardin B. Littlepage recalled that most of the spectators on shore cheered the occasion, he particularly remembered that "one man called out to us, 'Go on with your old metallic coffin! She will never amount to anything else!'" Anxiety, fear, seriousness, cockiness, and a host of other emotions inundated the crew as it now appeared to many aboard that their ship was destined for more than a trial trip.

The *Merrimac* seemed to crawl down the Elizabeth River as it moved at a speed of only four-and-one-half knots. Those aboard could not help but notice that she was slow, and they also saw, according to Engineer Ramsay, that she "steered so badly that, with her great length, it took from thirty to forty minutes to turn." This prompted one seaman to remark that "she was as unmanageable as a water-logged vessel."

Ultimately more than two hours elapsed before the ironclad passed the city of Norfolk and traveled the ten miles to Hampton Roads, the body of water where the James, Elizabeth, and Namesmond Rivers converge to flow into Chesapeake Bay. During the prolonged trip, Buchanan, knowing his true destination, ordered that the noon meal be served—many hours would pass before the ship's company would again have the opportunity to eat. The officers gathered at one end of their mess table in the wardroom to partake of their victuals, while at the opposite end Assistant Surgeon Algernon S. Garnett laid out bandages and surgical instruments. This left no doubt as to their true purpose.

As the *Merrimac* neared Craney Island shortly after noon, Buchanan had to take a towline from Lieutenant William H. Parker's tug *Beaufort*. Buchanan found that the ironclad's draft was so deep that her keel almost touched bottom. This limited the vessel's ability to turn; she also did not respond to her helm. In any case, by 12:30 the *Merrimac*, accompanied by the tug *Beaufort* and Lieutenant James W. Alexander's steam gunboat *Raleigh*, rounded Sewell's Point to the cheers of Confederate gunners at their batteries on shore. In front of the Confederate ships lay the Chesapeake Bay and a small portion of the Federal North Atlantic Blockading Squadron.

As the ironclad slowly continued towards the Federal fleet at anchor, Buchanan, through his spyglass, could count in the distance three coal ships and a hospital vessel; five tugboats and a side-wheel steamer; twelve gunboats mounting one to five guns; the screw frigates *Roanoke* and *Minnesota*; the storeship *Brandywine*, and the sailing frigates *St. Lawrence*, *Congress*, and *Cumberland*. This formidable detachment had 188 guns and more than 2,000 seamen, but its numbers made little difference; the Union forces were unprepared for the Confederate ironclad's arrival. Perhaps they had been lulled by the incessant rumors of the *Merrimac*'s failure, or maybe even desensitized by the constant reports of the ironclad's impend-

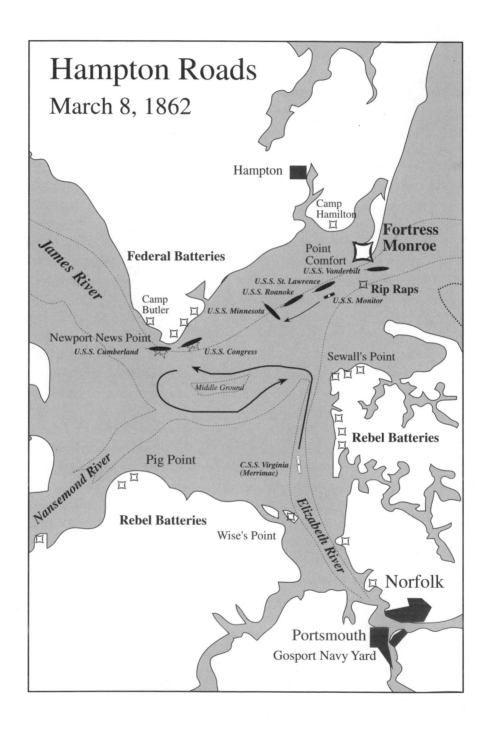

Hampton Roads
March 8, 1862

Hampton

Camp Hamilton

Fortress Monroe

Point Comfort

Federal Batteries

U.S.S. Vanderbilt

U.S.S. St. Lawrence
U.S.S. Roanoke

Camp Butler

U.S.S. Minnesota

Rip Raps

U.S.S. Monitor

James River

Newport News Point

U.S.S. Cumberland

U.S.S. Congress

Sewall's Point

Middle Ground

Rebel Batteries

Nansemond River

Pig Point

C.S.S. Virginia (Merrimac)

Elizabeth River

Rebel Batteries

Wise's Point

Norfolk

Portsmouth

Gosport Navy Yard

ing arrival. Regardless, the daily routine continued as usual within the Union fleet. It was Saturday—the traditional laundry day for the Navy—and washed white uniforms hung from the starboard riggings while blues dangled from the port. Lifeboats had been lowered from their booms, which indicated that men had been moving between ship and shore.

It appeared as if the Federal forces did not notice the approach of the Confederate ironclad and her entourage. Surgeon Dinwiddie Phillips remarked that "the curiosity of the *men* seemed to be somewhat aroused, and some of them collected together at the port-holes and on the forecastles to look at us, but for a long time no official notice was taken of us." Then all of a sudden, as he recounted, the smaller craft scrambled towards shore "like chickens on the approach of a hovering hawk." Signal flags were hoisted for the fleet. Dark black smoke began to bellow from the frigates *Minnesota* and *Roanoke* off Old Point. The sails of the *Cumberland* and *Congress* were unfurled as men scurried on deck to their battle stations.

Since Buchanan had now lost his element of surprise, he went below deck to inform his men of their mission. "In a few moments," he supposedly said, "you will have the long expected opportunity for showing your devotion to our cause. *Remember* that you are about to strike for your country, for your wives, your children, your homes." The men quickly moved to their battle stations, readied their guns, and waited as a solemn quiet, accentuated only by the rhythmic beating of the ship's engines, descended over the ironclad.

After passing through the mouth of the Elizabeth River, Buchanan chose to follow the south channel leading directly towards the *Cumberland* and *Congress* off Newport News. The commander notified his officers that they would first ram the stronger Union ship *Cumberland* and then turn on the weaker *Congress*. He contended that these ships would make easy prey since they were far removed from the remainder of the

Union fleet. These two ships were also stranded because of the lack of wind. Furthermore, since they were wooden they easily could be destroyed before the steam frigates *Minnesota* and *Roanoke* could come to their aid from Point Comfort.

Buchanan realized that he had surprised the Yankee fleet. A correspondent for the Boston *Journal* later claimed that "never has a brighter day smiled upon Old Virginia than last Saturday. The hours crept lazily along, and the sea and shore in this region saw nothing to vary the monotony of the scene." At 1:08 P.M. a lookout aboard the *Roanoke* off Fort Monroe spotted the Confederate ironclad and raised the signal for the fleet that reported the enemy's approach. But this was not new information. Some thirty minutes earlier the *Cumberland*, the *Congress*, and Federal forces further to the west at Newport News had been alerted to the ironclad's approach and had

Joseph B. Smith; the son of Admiral Joseph Smith, Joseph B. Smith was commissioned a midshipman in 1841; he served in various capacities at sea and saw duty during the Mexican War; he was promoted to passed midshipman in 1847, master in 1855, and lieutenant later that year; following the outbreak of the Civil War, Smith assumed command in early 1862 of the fifty-gun frigate U.S.S. *Congress*; on station in Hampton Roads off Newport News, Virginia, on 8 March 1862, the *Congress* came under attack from the Confederate ironclad *Virginia* (*Merrimac*); although Smith and his crew fought bravely, their wooden warship was no match for the armored *Virginia*; late in the day the *Congress* ran aground and was pounded by the Rebel ironclad; while directing an impossible defense, Smith was struck by a shell and killed instantly; his successor, Lieutenant Austin Pendergrast surrendered the ship, which was later destroyed; when Smith's father, then on duty at the Navy Department in Washington, received word of the *Congress'* surrender, he reportedly exclaimed "then Joe is dead."

already begun to prepare for an attack. Lieutenant Joseph B. Smith commanding the *Congress* had ordered his ship's decks cleared and his guns prepared for action. Executive officer Lieutenant George N. Morris commanding the *Cumberland*, which was anchored about three hundred yards off Newport News and two hundred yards north of her sister frigate, ordered that his ship's guns be readied and that sand be spread on the deck to soak up blood spilled during the battle. With these preparations made, they anxiously watched and waited.

Meanwhile Morris had called for the *Zouave*, a tugboat serving as tender and picket boat for the two frigates, to come alongside his frigate. The former Hudson River tug commanded by Acting Master Henry Reaney had been purchased, crew and all, to assist the North Atlantic Squadron's sailing frigates. It had not seen any fighting, nor did those aboard expect such duty. Nonetheless, Morris instructed Reaney to steam towards the mouth of the Namesmond River to see "what was causing the black smoke near Craney Island." After traveling only two miles Reaney witnessed "what to all appearances looked like the roof of a very big barn belching forth smoke as from a chimney on fire." He still was unsure of this strange vessel's purpose, until he saw "that she was flying the rebel flag, and immediately [he] decided that the long-talked-of *Merrimac* had come at last." Reaney's crew fired the tug's thirty-pounder Parrot rifle at the *Merrimac*; it was the first Federal SHOT of the day. The crew fired five more shots and then returned to assist the *Cumberland*.

While Reaney's *Zouave* towed the frigate into a position that allowed her broadside guns to face the approaching ironclad, shore batteries at Newport News and the guns of the *Congress* opened on the Confederate flotilla. Within minutes the *Cumberland*, now in position, also joined and the Union barrage became intense. The Confederate ironclad, still accompanied by the *Beaufort* and the *Raleigh*, slowly maneuvered towards the Federal force without firing a shot. At about

2 P.M. Parker's *Beaufort*, some three-quarters of a mile from the federal ships, fired the first Confederate volley of the day. Buchanan then gave his first and only order of the day when he raised the signal flag for "close action."

Buchanan had waited until the *Merrimac* was within close range before opening fire. Although this left the ironclad exposed to a constant barrage, Union shells seemed to bounce harmlessly off the ironclad's greased and casemated sides. Yet when Confederate cannon finally came to life, they exacted a heavy toll. The *Merrimac's* first shot struck the *Cumberland's* starboard quarter-rail, spraying the deck with splinters and wounding several of the marine guard—the first casualties of the battle. Lieutenant Thomas O. Selfridge, Jr., commanding the *Cumberland's* forward gun division, reported that "the groans of these men...as they were carried below, was something new." A second Confederate shot struck a Union cannon under the forward pivot. It disabled the gun and killed every man in its crew, except the gun captain who lost both arms and the powder boy who was slightly injured.

The *Cumberland* returned fire quickly "from the few guns she could bring to bear" on the *Merrimac*, but her shots did not damage the ironclad. It was truly the horrors of war as the Confederate ship's cannon fire dissected the wooden frigate leaving behind nothing but the wounded, who were sent below decks for medical care, and the dead, who were quickly thrown to the port side of the federal ship so the gun crews could continue their work. During the fray Selfridge noticed that "no one flinched, but went on loading and firing, taking the place of some comrade, killed or wounded, as they had been told to do." Even the sand that had been spread on the ship's deck to absorb blood could not soak up what seemed to be an unstoppable river. Nor could anything stem the fear or the anxiety that overtook those who watched, for what seemed like hours, as the Confederate ironclad moved ever so steadily towards the *Cumberland*.

At about 2:30 P.M. the *Merrimac* moved across the *Congress*'s line of fire and a blast of flame and smoke erupted from the Federal ship's broadside guns. Even though the Confederate ironclad was within very close range, the full force of the barrage seemed to inflict no damage whatsoever. One Union sailor remarked that the shots simply "struck and glanced off, having no more effect than peas from a pop-gun." Buchanan responded with a broadside of "hot shot," cannon balls heated red-hot in a furnace so as to set fire to ship timbers when they struck them. The hot shot had a terrible effect. One gunner aboard the *Congress* recalled, "all I remember about that broadside was of feeling something warm, and the next instant I found myself lying on the deck beside a number

Thomas Oliver Selfridge: born Massachusetts 1836; graduated U.S. Naval Academy first in his class of 1854; passed midshipman in 1856, master 1858, lieutenant 1860, he was present at the destruction of the Norfolk Navy Yard in 1861; commanded the forward battery on the U.S. frigate *Cumberland* in its battle with the *Merrimack* (*Virginia*) in March 1862; lieutenant commander 1862; joined the Mississippi River Squadron for the Vicksburg Campaign; during the Red River Expedition of 1864 he was instrumental in the dam building operations that allowed the Federal fleet to continue; with Admiral David Dixon Porter he joined the North Atlantic Squadron; he was conspicuously involved in the capture of Fort Fisher, North Carolina, in 1865; continuing in the U.S. Navy following the war, he was promoted to commander in 1869; participated in numerous surveys in Central and South America, including that of the Darien Isthmus (Panama) for which he received the Legion of Honor of France; captain

1881; commodore 1894; rear admiral 1896; retired 1898. Admiral Selfridge died in 1924; his memoirs were published the same year. Selfridge had a knack for being where the action was; he was involved in an amazing number of the Navy's most important events.

of my shipmates." One hot shot started a fire near the frigate's aft magazine which was quickly extinguished. Another struck a cabin on the ship's port side, igniting a fire which spread uncontrolled.

The *Merrimac* closed on the becalmed *Cumberland* amid the smoke and spray of battle. Buchanan had given strict instructions to his crew as to what to do when the ironclad rammed the Federal ship. He had informed engineer H. Ashton Ramsay not to wait for orders to reverse the ironclad's engines, but to do so when he first felt a collision. This would allow the Confederate vessel to back away as soon as possible without suffering extensive damage. All waited anxiously for that moment when suddenly, according to Jones, "the noise of crashing timbers was distinctly heard above the din of battle." The *Merrimac* then experienced a "slight" shock as the ship's iron ram tore a gaping hole, perhaps as large as seven feet wide, in the *Cumberland's* starboard side, just below the water line. The federal frigate "commenced to career" as brown water gushed into the hole.

For a moment no one realized that unless the *Merrimac* immediately pulled away, the weight of the sinking *Cumberland* could also force the Confederate ship to the bottom of the bay. But Ramsay soon understood the danger as the Federal frigate pushed the Confederate ironclad down at the bow. Although Ramsay had followed instructions and reversed the engines as soon as the ships collided, the ships seemed to be stuck together. "The engines labored, and the vessel was shaken in every fiber," Ramsay recalled, but the ironclad could not pull away. The engineer feared the worse, and, to compound matters, he then heard a thunderous explosion that sounded like a ruptured boiler. Actually a shell had exploded in the *Merrimac's* smokestack raining fragments onto the engine room floor but otherwise causing little damage. Just as it appeared that the ironclad would also find a watery grave, the tide forced the ironclad around until she lay parallel to the

Cumberland. A fortuitous wave then rolled the Yankee ship, allowing the *Merrimac* to break free. The Confederate ship had finally escaped, although without her iron prow, which had broken off in the *Cumberland.* The *Merrimac,* despite this damage, could continue the fight; the Federal frigate was mortally wounded.

For nearly thirty minutes the two ships had maintained a continuous fire as the ironclad attempted to break free. One disheartened Union sailor remembered that their shots simply struck "the inclined sides of the *Merrimac,* bounded up and flew over, dropping into the water beyond." Confederate shots, however, passed through the *Cumberland's* wooden side, "throwing splinters and fragments of iron among our men on the gun deck, and producing," as forward gun commander Moses Stuyvesant observed, "a scene of carnage and destruc-

The *Merrimac* ramming the U.S.S. *Cumberland*

tion never to be recalled without horror." Below decks water continued to pour into the frigate's hold pulling her bow ever downward. Although the *Cumberland* was sinking, her crew continued firing and refused to surrender. Lieutenant Jones recounted that the Union ship "fought her guns gallantly as long as they were above water. She went down bravely, with her colors flying." Shortly after 3:30 P.M., the *Cumberland* lurched forward one last time and descended into the dark Chesapeake waters. When the ship's hull settled on the muddy bottom, the upper portions of her masts protruded above the water. This fortunately provided refuge for many sailors who had been unable to escape as the ship went down.

As the smoke cleared, Buchanan ascertained his position and decided to proceed against the *Congress*. But his ship was out of position to initiate an attack. Moreover, the ebb tide, as well as the ironclad's sluggish steering and poor speed, forced Buchanan to steam upriver before he could turn to attack. As the ironclad moved away Union seamen aboard the *Congress* "gave three cheers, under the belief that [the Confederate ship was] running away." The cheering abruptly stopped when the ironclad made its wide turn and came back downstream.

Lieutenant Joseph Smith, the recently appointed commanding officer of the *Congress*, could only watch as the ironclad mutilated his sister ship. He wanted to come to the *Cumberland*'s aid but had been occupied during the battle with Commander John R. Tucker's Confederate James River Squadron, the *Patrick Henry*, the *Teaser*, and the *Jamestown*, as well as with Confederate gunboats *Beaufort* and *Raleigh*. Smith's able defense was encouraging given the fate of the *Cumberland*. Even more promising was that the Union ships *Roanoke*, *Minnesota*, and *St. Lawrence* were steaming to aid Smith's frigate. Unfortunately, all three of these ships ran aground on shallows in the middle of the bay before they could be of assistance. Despite being grounded they continued to fire on the *Merrimac* with whatever guns they could bring to bear.

Smith, suddenly realizing his limited options, had the ship's sails unfurled, and ordered the tug *Zouave* to move the ship towards shore. This seemed a curious decision, but considering what had happened to the *Cumberland*, Smith at least wanted to give his vessel a fighting chance. The frigate could continue to fire its guns even if she sank in the shallow waters off Newport News. More importantly, Smith believed that the shoals would prevent the *Merrimac* from ramming his ship.

By the time the Confederate ironclad had completed its turn, the *Congress* was well near shore. But as luck would have it, the current turned the ship, leaving only two of her guns in a position to aim at the Confederate ironclad. Although the shallow water prevented Buchanan from bringing the *Merrimac* within point-blank range (he remained two hundred yards off the Federal ship), the tide allowed the Confederates to position the ironclad out of the Union frigate's line of fire. Once that happened the *Merrimac* easily dismembered the *Congress* shot by shot.

Each of the ironclad's broadsides devastated the *Congress*. The pilothouse and figurehead were blown away immediately. The carnage was so gruesome, according to Reaney, that blood from the frigate's deck ran "onto [the *Zouave*'s] deck like water on a wash-deck morning." The gallant Lieutenant Smith was suddenly struck by a shell that ripped off his head and a portion of his shoulder—his rank insignia fell to the deck. Within ten minutes of the first broadside the frigate's stern had been destroyed, several fires had broken out, and the *Congress* was helpless against the *Merrimac*. Compounding the Union ship's problem was that the other Confederate ships made it hard for small boats to ferry the wounded Union sailors ashore. Lieutenant Austin Pendergrast, who had replaced Smith as commander, consulted with the other surviving officers aboard before concluding that surrender offered the only alternative to annihilation. At about 4:45 P.M., after enduring almost an hour of bombardment, Pendergrast ordered the *Congress*'s colors struck, and a white surrender flag raised.

Buchanan felt relieved when he saw the white flag. He knew his younger brother, McKean Buchanan, was serving as paymaster aboard the *Congress*, and the ship's surrender gave the Confederate commander hope that he had survived; McKean was, in fact, one of the few to survive the Confederate attack. Coming out onto the *Merrimac*'s deck, Buchanan instructed Lieutenant Parker of the *Beaufort* to scuttle the Federal ship, to release the seamen, and to bring the officers aboard the *Merrimac* as prisoners. When Parker approached the *Congress* he saw first-hand the destruction that had been wrought on the frigate. "The carnage was frightful," he later recalled. He saw the wounded, many of whom were dismembered and disfigured, and dead bodies, thrown into piles as if they were wood. He also learned that Joseph Smith, his Naval Academy friend and classmate, had died during the battle. After meeting Lieutenant Pendergrast, Parker informed the Union officer that he should relinquish his sidearm and sword as was customary at a surrender. While Pendergrast returned aboard the burning ship to find his weapons, Union sharp-shooters on shore opened fire, killing several Confederate sailors, wounding Parker in the knee, and forcing a hasty retreat before the *Congress* had been fired.

Buchanan had been watching from aboard the *Merrimac* and wondered why the Union warship had not been destroyed. At first he thought that Parker had deliberately failed to complete his mission. Buchanan became furious, as he could not see that Union soldiers on shore were leveling a devastating fire. Lieutenant Robert Minor, who had already offered to board and burn the *Congress*, again volunteered his services, and Captain Buchanan readily accepted. Taking the ironclad's last small boat, Minor and a small group of men rowed towards the Federal frigate. But just as Minor neared the *Congress*, he and two other men were struck by shots from Union soldiers on shore. All aboard the small boat would have

probably been killed had the *Teaser* not steamed by and res-
cued them. This time Buchanan saw events as they evolved,
and his observation was confirmed by a signal from the
Teaser. Seething with anger, he yelled, "destroy that — —
ship!" He then took a rifle and began to fire at the sharpshoot-
ers on shore. Almost instantly, hot shot and shell gushed from
the *Merrimac* and struck the helpless *Congress*. Only moments
later, Buchanan was shot in the leg and had to be carried
below to his quarters. The Confederate commander immediately called Jones to his wardroom, and told him to continue
fighting as long as the men and light endured.

According to wounded Lieutenant Minor, "brave, cool,
determined old Jones fought the action out in his quiet way,
giving them thunder all the time." It was apparent that Jones
was not as aggressive or flamboyant as Buchanan, but he
nonetheless continued the Confederate attack with the same
intensity. By 5:00 P.M. the *Congress* was fully ablaze and out
of commission. Turning his attention to the grounded
Minnesota, Jones realized that the ironclad's deep draft would
prohibit a close-in attack, a view which the pilots aboard the
ironclad confirmed. With darkness approaching, Jones decided
to steam towards the Elizabeth River. Jones later reported that
"we fought until it was so dark that we could not see to point
the guns with accuracy." By 6:30 P.M. the *Merrimac* had fired
her last shot for the day. Ninety minutes later the ironclad had
anchored under Confederate guns on Sewell's Point.

Jones's job had just started when the *Merrimac* dropped
anchor. As acting commander he had to make sure that the
bodies of the two men killed in action were taken ashore. The
eight men who had been wounded during the day had to be
removed by Surgeon Phillips and Federal prisoners had to be
turned over to Major William Norris of the Signal Corps to be
taken to the Norfolk hospital. Meanwhile the cooks and stew-
ards had their own duties, which delayed their serving dinner
until almost midnight. The *Merrimac* had to be inspected for

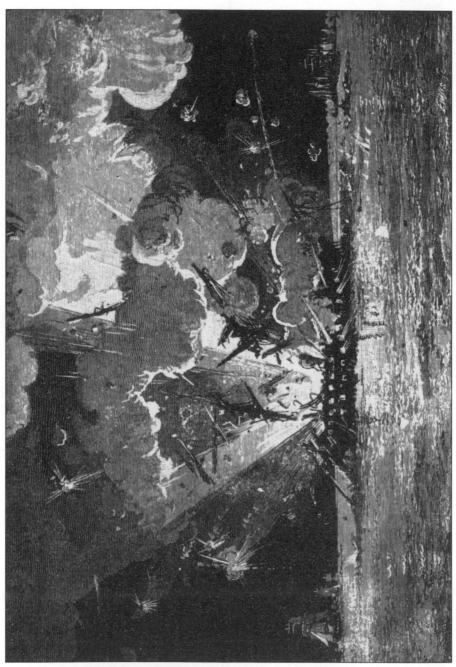

The explosion of U.S.S. *Congress*

damage and the report of the day's events drafted. At 12:30 A.M., about the same time that Jones went to bed, the *Congress*, which had been burning since the afternoon, exploded in what one witness on shore described as "one of the grandest episodes of this splendid yet somber drama."

As the *Congress* burned and sank into the Chesapeake waters, a Confederate pilot aboard the *Merrimac* noticed "a strange-looking craft, brought out in bold relief by the brilliant light of the burning ship, which he at once proclaimed to be the Ericsson." The pilot was correct, for when the sun rose on the following morning the *Monitor* lay at anchor near the grounded *Minnesota*. This day, Sunday, March 9, 1862, would differ starkly from the previous one.

5

"ONE OF THE GREATEST NAVAL ENGAGEMENTS"

At Washington, D.C., early on that same Sunday morning, Secretary of the Navy Gideon Welles read a telegraph dispatch from Major General John Wool, Union commander at Fort Monroe. The message recounted the naval battle of the previous day in Hampton Roads and the news was distressing at best. Just as Welles finished, he received a summons to appear immediately at the White House. Apparently President Lincoln had also received a report of the battle, and the Cabinet would meet to discuss the emergency.

When Welles arrived at the Executive Mansion he found Secretary of State William Seward, Secretary of the Treasury Salmon P. Chase, and War Secretary Edwin Stanton already present. Moments later Lincoln sent for Captain John A. Dahlgren and Army Quartermaster General Montgomery C.

Meigs. To the surprise of all present, they learned that the battle in Hampton Roads had lasted only five hours, during which the Confederate ironclad had sunk two frigates, damaged a third warship, killed almost three hundred Federal sailors, and wounded one hundred more. The *Merrimac* had wreaked devastation on the Union squadron and had suffered virtually no damage. Welles recalled that Stanton "was at times almost frantic." The news disturbed the secretary greatly and he proclaimed hysterically that the ironclad "would destroy every vessel in the service, could lay every city on the coast under contribution,...could come up the Potomac and disperse Congress, destroy the Capitol and public buildings." Even worse, Stanton contended that "she might go to New York and Boston and destroy those cities." As he vented his alarm and paced around the room, Stanton frequently looked out the White House window, as if he expected to see the Confederate ironclad in the Potomac River.

All present looked to Welles for reassurance and answers. Yet the navy secretary could only tell them that the *Monitor* had been sent to the Chesapeake, and that the *Merrimac's* draft would prohibit her from steaming up the Potomac. While these assurances apparently eased Seward's misgivings, they did nothing to calm Stanton. When the meeting concluded Lincoln went to the navy yard to talk at length with Dahlgren, while Welles left to speak with Commodore Joseph Smith, father of Lieutenant Smith who had died aboard the *Congress*. Stanton departed for his office and immediately sent messages to the governors of New York, Massachusetts, and Maine, warning them of the *Merrimac's* impending arrival. Later that afternoon the Cabinet reconvened to discuss what further action should be taken. They were unaware that events in the Chesapeake Bay had already decided the issue for them.

Only a heavy fog, which hovered above the waters of the Chesapeake, dampened the enthusiasm of Confederates that Sunday morning. "That Morrow! How anxiously we waited for it," remarked one eyewitness. Yet "how much we feared its results!" Anticipation had kept virtually everyone awake during the night. Surgeon Phillips declared that "we had scarcely been asleep" when suddenly the boatswaim's pipe awakened the crew. Although the sun had not yet risen, the men promptly dressed and sat down to a hearty breakfast accompanied by two jiggers of whiskey per man. Many gorged themselves as if it was their last meal; they realized that some might not return, and they knew that in the heat of battle they would have no opportunity to eat.

After breakfast Surgeon Phillips escorted a remonstrating Captain Buchanan ashore, while Jones prepared the vessel for the day's action. Buchanan did not want to leave his ship at this climactic moment, but Phillips had impressed upon the captain that his departure would provide needed space for the wounded he expected. Buchanan reluctantly agreed. Phillips soon returned to the ironclad, and as he rowed a boat around the *Merrimac*, he discovered what Jones had written about the previous night. The ship had ninety-eight dents from enemy missiles, and the smokestack had so many holes that it "would have permitted a flock of crows to fly through it without inconvenience." Moreover, Phillips saw what Jones had been unable to see—the iron prow on the bow had been ripped off, leaving a hole through which water slowly seeped. Regardless of what Phillips saw, however, Jones knew the *Merrimac* was still seaworthy and had a job to finish.

When the sun rose shortly after 6:30 A.M., Jones noticed through the misty fog that the *Minnesota* was still stranded. He ordered engineer Ramsay to make steam, weigh anchor, and proceed into Hampton Roads. Jones would first finish off the *Minnesota* and then turn to the remainder of the Federal fleet in the Bay. On this day, Jones's ironclad would be accompanied by the *Patrick Henry*, the *Jamestown*, and the *Teaser*. And once again, the banks surrounding the Bay would be lined with spectators, as all anticipated a repeat of the previous day's activities. But as Confederate ships moved into Hampton Roads, Jones saw that the *Minnesota* was not alone. During the night a strange-looking ship—the *Monitor*—had come to her aid. It did not look like a formidable weapon but rather resembled a "large cheese box." Even so, the "iron battery" did not dampen Confederate morale nor did anyone think it would keep the *Merrimac* from finishing her business.

The *Monitor* had arrived in the Chesapeake Bay the previous evening at about 9:00 P.M. and anchored off the stranded *Minnesota* shortly after midnight. Engineer Alban C. Stimers recalled that the ironclad's appearance did little to revive the "gloomy and down hearted. Our arrival gave but little confidence as we were an experimental test of an untried invention." One Union sailor mourned, "How insignificant [the

Alban C. Stimers: Born New York 1827; Stimers entered the U.S. Navy as an assistant engineer in 1849 and by 1861 had achieved the rank of chief engineer; selected to assist John Ericsson in the construction of the experimental ironclad *Monitor*, Stimers was largely responsible for keeping the project on schedule; when the *Monitor* received orders to proceed to Hampton Roads off the Virginia

coast, Stimers went along in an unofficial capacity but was soon pressed into service, restoring the boilers and blowers to working order after the ironclad almost foundered at sea; during the 9 March 1862 battle with the Confederate ironclad *Virginia* (*Merrimac*), Stimers operated the *Monitor's* rotating turret and directed a gun crew; after the famous battle, Stimers returned to New York to assist Ericsson in the development of *Passaic* class monitors; after being detailed to service the monitor fleet during Admiral S.F. DuPont's unsuccessful attack on Charleston Harbor in 1863, Stimers returned to New York to supervise the construction of the *Casco* class ironclads; charged with serious

production errors during this project, he was relegated to a lesser role for the remainder of the war; he resigned in August 1865; Stimers worked as a civilian engineer until his death 1876.

Monitor] looked." But others found the new arrival more encouraging. Even though the ironclad did not appear to be a menacing weapon, Thomas Rae aboard the *Minnesota* recalled "what a jump our hearts gave"; and the frigate's sailors "gave a cheer that might have been heard in Richmond."

Worden's crew, like the Confederates aboard the *Merrimac*, did not get much sleep, as they turned in at about five o'clock Sunday morning. Besides, the Union sailors had experienced a trying forty-eight hours of stormy seas during their trip from New York. Those who did manage to nod off were awakened for breakfast about two hours later. While they ate, some noticed heavy black smoke erupting from the Confederate position two miles away. It was obvious that the ironclad and her consorts were beginning to move, probably, as most believed, in the direction of the *Minnesota*.

Worden received news of the *Merrimac*'s approach and steamed alongside the stranded Union frigate. Captain

Gershom J. Van Brunt: Born New Jersey 1798; Van Brunt entered the U.S. Navy as a midshipman in 1818 and served against pirates in the Caribbean; promoted to lieutenant in 1827, he became a commander in 1846; he commanded the brig *Etna* in the Gulf of Mexico during the Mexican War and was elevated to captain in 1855; Van Brunt commanded the frigate *Minnesota* during the famous battle between the U.S.S. *Monitor* and C.S.S. *Virginia* (*Merrimac*); after the *Virginia* destroyed the *Cumberland* and *Congress* on 8 March 1862, the *Minnesota* ran aground early the next day and awaited a similar fate; Van Brunt worked feverishly to refloat his ship and give battle but the ironclad *Monitor* took up the fight and the frigate was saved; promoted to commodore in July 1862, Van Brunt was retired the following April; he died at Dedham, Massachusetts, in December 1863.

Gershom J. Van Brunt of the *Minnesota* had spent the night trying to refloat his ship; all extraneous equipment and materials had been thrown overboard and men had been removed, all to no avail. Worden knew that the Confederate ships would not arrive for some time, so he asked Van Brunt if the *Monitor* could be of assistance to the frigate. Van Brunt responded that he would destroy the *Minnesota* if he could not refloat her. After all, he asserted, "the idea of assistance or protection being offered to the huge thing by the little pygmy at her side seemed absolutely ridiculous."

While Van Brunt tried unsuccessfully to refloat the Federal frigate, Worden prepared his ironclad to meet the Confederate attack. Suddenly, a whizzing shell flew over the *Monitor* and struck the *Minnesota*, prompting sailors standing on the Yankee ironclad's deck to hurry below and prepare for battle. According to Paymaster Keeler, after the Confederate shot, "the most profound silence reigned." "The suspense was awful," for the crew "were enclosed in what we supposed to be an impenetrable armour—we knew that a powerful foe was about to meet us—ours was an untried experiment & the enemy's first fire might make it a coffin for us all." Within the ironclad's shell it was dark and quiet, and at any moment all aboard expected that a Confederate shell would strike their vessel with unspeakable consequences.

The men aboard the *Monitor* heard three more shots hurtling toward the *Minnesota*, before the Union frigate responded with her first broadside. With this exchange of fire the battle began. The *Monitor* raised anchor and began to station herself between the approaching Confederate ship and the stranded Union frigate. As he moved into position, Worden ordered Lieutenant Samuel Dana Greene, a twenty-one-year-old Marylander, to "commence firing." Greene's gun crew loaded a cannon and the lieutenant pulled the lanyard. Quartermaster Peter Truscott, alleging that the shot startled the Confederates, declared that "you can see surprise on a ship just the same as you can see it in a human being, and there was surprise all over the *Merrimac*." Stimers proclaimed that the *Monitor*'s first shot "no doubt greatly astonished" the *Merrimac*.

Jones as well as others aboard the Rebel ironclad were astonished to discover the *Monitor*'s presence. After the previous day, no one thought that a Union commander would sacrifice his ship to protect a doomed wooden frigate. Moreover, most were unsure of the *Monitor*'s mission; some believed she was but a watertank supplying the frigate, an immobile iron battery, or even the boilers being removed from the stranded *Minnesota*. No one expected the *Monitor* to come out as "David goes out to meet Goliath." But all Confederate doubt was removed when the Union ironclad's first shot struck the *Merrimac*.

Jones initially ignored the *Monitor*'s presence and continued to advance towards the stranded *Minnesota*. But when the pilots informed Jones that the ironclad could not close on the frigate because of shallow water, the lieutenant chose instead to fight the *Monitor*.

It was now about 8:45 A.M. as the two ships closed to within fifty yards, circling one another while trying to gain an advantageous position. The *Merrimac*'s deep draft, poor steering, and slow speed left her at a disadvantage. The *Monitor*, with her shallow draft and efficient engines, was able to steam circles around the Confederate vessel. The ships moved as close as a few feet from one another and as far apart as one hundred yards, all the while maintaining a constant fire. The eleven-inch solid shot from the *Monitor*'s guns dented the Rebel vessel's iron casemate and splintered her oak backing. In addition to the pounding of iron on iron, Confederate sailors had to contend with crackling boiler fires that produced intense heat, smoke from fires and cannon, and the loud continual beat of the *Merrimac*'s steam engines. It was a frantic experience, as the men soon realized that their efforts had lit-

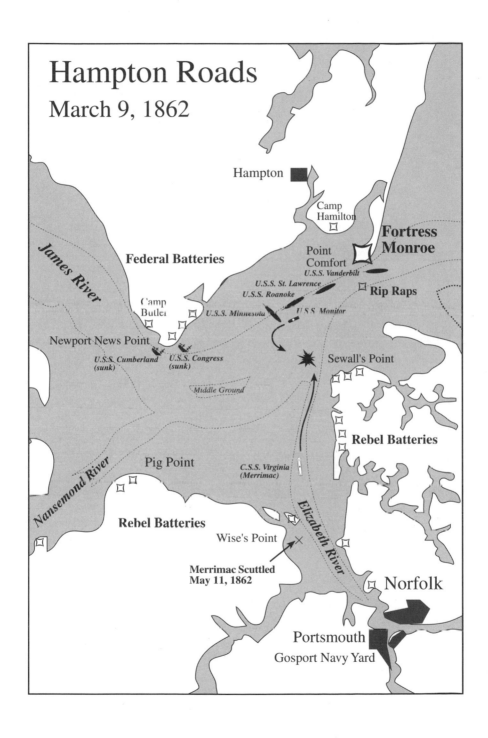

Hampton Roads
March 9, 1862

Hampton

Camp
Hamilton

**Fortress
Monroe**

Point
Comfort

Federal Batteries

U.S.S. Vanderbilt

U.S.S. St. Lawrence
U.S.S. Roanoke

Rip Raps

James River

Camp
Butler

U.S.S. Minnesota

U.S.S. Monitor

Newport News Point

U.S.S. Cumberland
(sunk)

U.S.S. Congress
(sunk)

Sewall's Point

Middle Ground

Rebel Batteries

Pig Point

C.S.S. Virginia
(Merrimac)

Nansemond River

Rebel Batteries

Wise's Point

**Merrimac Scuttled
May 11, 1862**

Elizabeth River

Norfolk

Portsmouth
Gosport Navy Yard

Encounter: The *Monitor* and the *Merrimac* at close range

tle effect on their adversary. It was certainly not reminiscent of yesterday's encounter.

Confederate morale was beginning to wane as the exploding shells from the *Merrimac*, according to Lieutenant Eggleston, simply "burst into fragments against [the *Monitor*'s] turret." Meanwhile, Union spirits improved as Lieutenant Greene reported that Confederate shells had dented but not penetrated the *Monitor*'s armor. When Greene fearfully relayed his observations to Stimers, the engineer responded, "Of course it made a big dent—that is just what we expected, but what do you care about that as long as it keeps out the shot?" This reassurance greatly revived Union morale, after which, Greene reported, "a look of confidence passed over the men's faces." Before long sailors aboard the *Monitor* were confident that the *Merrimac* would quickly be humbled.

At about 10:30 A.M., after about two hours of almost continuous combat, disaster struck the *Merrimac*. With all the circling and maneuvering, the pilots aboard the Confederate ironclad became disoriented and allowed her to run aground. With her twenty-two-foot draft, the *Merrimac* became mired in the muddy bottom of the Chesapeake Bay, helpless against the *Monitor*. Jones hurried to the engine room to impress upon Ramsay the urgency they faced. For the next fifteen minutes the *Monitor* maintained a ceaseless fire against the Rebel monster, which, engineer Ramsay proclaimed, "began to sound every chink in our armour." Surgeon Phillips remarked that the *Monitor* appeared to circle "like a fierce dog" seeking an opening. Although five or six short-range Union shots cracked the iron sheathing and bent the timbers behind, Jones could be thankful that his ironclad's armor held.

Meanwhile, Ramsay did everything within his power to refloat the ship. He burned any combustibles, including oiled cotton waste and turpentine-coated wood splinters, that could increase the ship's steam. Even with higher pressure, which turned the ship's propeller at a feverish pace and churned the muddy Chesapeake waters, the ironclad remained grounded. Helpless sailors could do nothing to alleviate their condition and many felt their hearts sink lower with each passing minute. Then all of a sudden the ironclad staggered backwards, pulling free and moving into deeper water.

Jones scurried through the gun deck commanding his men to resume their cannonade. Lieutenant Eggleston, however, instructed his men to rest. When Jones asked the lieutenant, "Why are you not firing, sir," Eggleston simply responded that it would be a waste of precious powder and ammunition. Moreover, he claimed, "I can do her just about as much damage by snapping my thumb at her every two minutes and a half." Jones realized what Eggleston meant. The Confederate cannon could not penetrate the *Monitor*'s turret or iron sheathing, nor could the *Merrimac*'s armor continue to withstand the pounding of the enemy's guns. Jones concluded that his only recourse was to ram the *Monitor* or "run her down." He did not realize, however, that the *Merrimac*'s iron prow had been lost the day before.

The commands, "'Back the engines'—now 'go ahead'—now 'hard a-starboard the helm'—now 'hard a-port'" resounded through the *Merrimac* as Jones tried to position his ironclad for ramming. Aboard the *Monitor*, Worden realized Jones's intentions, tried to avoid a direct collision, and instructed Greene to continue firing on the Confederate vessel. As Keeler hurried to the gun turret with Worden's order, he knew that "this was the critical moment, one that [he] had feared from the beginning of the fight." Fortunately, Jones's ship was too large, too unresponsive, and too slow to build up the speed necessary to inflict severe damage on the Union vessel. Moreover, shortly before the two ships made contact, Worden turned the helm hard, away from the *Merrimac*. "At that moment of terrible suspense," Keeler recounted, the Union warship suffered only "a heavy jar nearly throwing us from our feet." But nothing had penetrated the half-inch iron hull, and no water flooded into the ironclad. Keeler rejoiced, "We were safe."

The two ships had been firing at one another while they prepared for and after they had made contact. Greene had discharged his guns at close range, stunning Confederate sailors aboard the *Merrimac*, knocking them from their feet, as well as leaving them dazed and bleeding from their noses, mouths, and ears. Return fire struck outside the *Monitor's* turret near where engineer Stimers, acting master Louis Stodder, and gunner Peter Truscott stood. The force of the blow knocked all three to the deck. Stimers was shaken but quickly jumped up; Stodder "was flung by the concussion clean over both guns to the floor"; Truscott "dropped over like a dead man." None of the three suffered permanent injury, but all became acutely aware of the force they confronted.

It was at about this time that Worden withdrew to shallow water to replenish his ammunition stocks within the turret. To do so, hatchways between the turret and main deck had to be aligned and this could only be accomplished when the turret remained stationary. As the *Monitor* pulled away from the battle, Confederates believed that she had given up the fight. Even Van Brunt aboard the *Minnesota* thought that the ironclad had retreated. In fact, Henry Reaney recalled, "every preparation was being made to abandon [the *Minnesota*] and blow her up."

During the fifteen minutes in which the *Monitor* replenished her ammunition supply, Jones turned his attention to the *Minnesota*. The gun crews aboard the *Merrimac* had been firing at the stranded frigate at every opportune moment. Jones later defended his actions against claims that during the day his ship had actually fired more shots at the *Minnesota* than it had fired at the *Monitor* by stating that his guns could not seriously harm the *Monitor*. One shot from Jones's barrage started a fire aboard the *Minnesota*, while another struck and destroyed the nearby tug *Dragon*. Other than this, the Confederates inflicted little damage that Sunday.

Monitor vs. Merrimac, with surrounding vignettes

CALORIC ENGINE

SECTIONAL VIEW—MERRIMAC

WARD ROOM (MONITOR)

WHEEL HOUSE (MONITOR)

ENGINE ROOM (MONITOR)

MONITOR

Some of Jones's officers suggested that they attempt to board the Union ironclad when the two engaged again. Jones agreed to the proposal, which entailed the use of sledge hammers and spikes to wedge the turret. Once the turret had been "choked," the vessel would be lashed to the *Merrimac*, and towed back to Norfolk. Jones's crew readied their cutlasses, pikes, and pistols as a "breathless hush" pervaded the ship. All waited for "a single stroke of the bell"—the order to board the enemy vessel. But before any such attempt could occur, the *Monitor* steamed by the Confederate ship and the opportunity passed. In any case, Worden had prepared for the possibility of being boarded by readying hand grenades to be used against such an attack.

Worden had decided, as the *Monitor*'s turret was being reloaded, that he should ram the *Merrimac*. His ironclad was faster and more maneuverable, so he believed he could hit the Confederate ship on her stern—her most vulnerable spot. The collision would damage the *Merrimac*'s rudder and propeller, leaving the Confederate ship at the whim of the currents or even worse, at the mercy of the Union Navy. Worden was able to maneuver his vessel to Jones's stern and closed at full speed for the *Merrimac*'s hull. At the last moment, the *Monitor*'s steering failed and the ironclad missed its target by only a few feet. Had Worden's vessel struck the *Merrimac*, the effect would have been devastating.

Jones had ordered his gunners to concentrate on the *Monitor*'s pilothouse as the enemy ironclad approached, and at about 11:30 A.M., when the two ships were within twenty yards, Jones opened fire at point-blank range. A blast from the *Merrimac*'s pivot gun struck one of the sight-holes on the *Monitor*'s pilothouse. Paymaster Keeler remembered, "a flash of light & a cloud of smoke filled the house." Then suddenly Worden grabbed his face, exclaiming "I am blind." Apparently the explosion had sent particles of paint and iron through the slits in the pilothouse and into Worden's face. Now, covered with powder and iron, and bleeding profusely from his face, Worden stumbled backwards. Officers quickly gathered around and questioned him about his condition. It was soon obvious that he was unable to continue his command. Meanwhile, Quartermaster Peter Williams had, without orders, turned the *Monitor*'s helm away from the *Merrimac*. For the next twenty minutes, while Union officers attended Worden, the *Monitor* moved away from the *Merrimac*. Although no one realized it at the time, the battle between the two ironclads had ended.

Lieutenant Greene, hovering over Worden, asked his commander what action the *Monitor* should take. Worden responded, "I leave it with you, do what you think best...Save the *Minnesota* if you can." Greene escorted Worden back to his cabin before returning to examine the damage to the *Monitor*'s pilothouse. The executive officer realized that should another shot strike the pilothouse, it would probably penetrate the iron casing and all inside would be killed. Even so, his officers had conferred and agreed that the *Monitor*, which had moved well into shoal waters by this time, should resume the battle. Greene concurred, but by the time the *Monitor* had reversed its course, the *Merrimac* was steaming towards Norfolk.

Confederates, including Jones, believed that the *Monitor* had retreated from the fight. "The fact is," one sailor claimed, "the *Monitor* was afraid of the" *Merrimac*. Others, however, thought it was but a Union trick to lure the Confederate ship aground in shallow water. Jones watched with amazement because "the *Monitor* appeared unharmed," yet she still retreated. As the Federal ironclad withdrew, Jones prepared to move against the *Minnesota*. At this point, however, a new problem presented itself. Pilots informed Jones that the tide was receding and that the ship could not move within a mile of the stranded Yankee frigate. Moreover, the water was just barely deep enough to allow Jones's ship to cross the sandbar at the mouth of the Elizabeth River. If the *Merrimac* did not retire towards Norfolk soon, the ship would be forced by the ebbing tide to remain in the Bay until the following morning. Jones then asked his fellow officers: "The *Monitor* has given up the fight and run into shoal water; the pilots cannot take us any nearer to the *Minnesota*; this ship is leaking from the loss of her prow; the men are exhausted by being so long at their guns;...I propose to return to Norfolk for repairs. What is your opinion?" After some discussion the officers agreed to return to the Gosport Navy Yard. In his official report Jones concluded, "had there been any sign of the *Monitor*'s willingness to renew the contest we would have remained to fight her." Just as Jones had interpreted Worden's withdrawal as a retreat, Greene concluded that it was the *Merrimac* that had deserted the fight. In fact, both sides misinterpreted the actions of the other and while both thought they had won, neither actually had.

As the two antagonists moved away from one another, men aboard both ironclads came to their respective decks for fresh air. For most involved, it had been a long trying day that seemed to have produced little result. The two ironclads had sparred for almost four hours and had done minimal damage to each other. The engagement did provide a tactical victory for the Federals as the *Monitor* had fulfilled her primary objective of saving the frigate *Minnesota*. The battle allowed the Confederates to maintain strategic control over Hampton Roads and the James River; Union forces could not move against Norfolk, and General George B. McClellan had to modify his spring 1862 campaign against Richmond. Although many realized that neither side could claim outright victory, they did acknowledge that history had been made. One Union soldier ashore remarked that the battle was "one of the greatest Naval Engagements that has ever ocured [*sic*] since the Beginning of the world."

By 4:00 P.M. the *Merrimac* was back in dry dock at the Gosport Navy Yard. Jones and his fellow sailors had received a hero's welcome as they steamed up the Elizabeth River. Crowds had lined the shore and had shouted cheers of praise.

As the ironclad was being secured, Jones mustered his crew and praised their bravery and the men responded to the accolades with three hearty cheers for their commander. Jones then dismissed them, allowing most to go ashore to visit family and friends. They were heroes for the moment, but several, including Jones, felt intense disappointment. Later that evening, recalling the day's events, Jones told Major William Norris: "The destruction of those wooden vessels was a matter of course especially so, being at anchor, but in not capturing that ironclad, I feel as if we had done nothing." But Jones, Ramsay, Worden, Greene, and all aboard both vessels had done something that transcended the results of this particular encounter. They had helped revolutionize naval warfare and the world would never again be the same.

6

"IRON WILL BE KING
OF THE SEAS"

At noon on Monday, March 10, 1862, the assistant rector of
Trinity Episcopal Church in Portsmouth, Virginia, Reverend J.
H. D. Wingfield, offered a service of thanksgiving and praise
aboard the *Merrimac*'s gundeck. Discounting news of
Confederate setbacks in other theaters of combat, Wingfield
uplifted his audience. "How suddenly all is changed! The sun-
shine of a favoring Providence beams upon every countenance!
Our arms have been marvelously crowned with a brilliant suc-
cess!" Praising those to whom he spoke, he concluded: "The
happy result is that the fierce weapons of our insolent
invaders are broken; the enemies' mighty ships are spoiled;
our long-blockaded port is once again thrown open, and our
hearts are filled with joy and gratitude at the great and glori-
ous victory!" Yet the battle during the two previous days had

not given the Confederates such a victory. It had ended in a draw at best.

After the sermon, the seamen disembarked and the *Merrimac* went into dry dock for repairs. During the next three weeks mechanics worked day and night to replace the cracked outer iron plates, and to restore the damaged timbers behind. Port shutters, two rifled guns, a new anchor, a stronger iron prow, and a host of other improvements were added. Furthermore, solid iron shot, to be used in the next engagement with the *Monitor*, replaced the ineffectual exploding shells in the *Merrimac*'s magazines. These repairs and additions, according to many, would make the *Merrimac* a more formidable weapon. But even so, she still was not a sea-going vessel.

By April 4, 1862, although not completely finished, the ironclad prepared to leave dry dock. During the down time, command of the *Merrimac* had devolved on Commodore Josiah Tattnall, a sixty-seven-year-old Georgian who had joined the U.S. Navy in 1812, served in the Mexican War, and commanded the East Indian Squadron. Buchanan, still suffering from the wound he received during the battle, had to be replaced. Many thought that command would fall to Jones since he had gallantly finished the battle against the *Monitor*, but the seniority system meant that Jones was too young for permanent command of the vessel. In any case, Secretary Mallory had the utmost confidence in Tattnall. Although others thought the Georgia officer was too old and infirm for such an arduous position, Mallory nonetheless instructed him "not [to] hesitate or wait for order, but strike when, how, and where your judgment may dictate."

The *Merrimac* did not move against the Federal forces in Hampton Roads until mid-April, and only then in response to information that General George McClellan intended to use the nearby York River as an invasion route against Richmond. Learning this, Tattnall knew that he would have to confront the

Monitor, which had remained in a defensive position under the guns of Fort Monroe during late March and early April 1862, before he could steam to aid Confederate soldiers in their defense against McClellan. Calling a council of junior officers,

Josiah Tattnall: Born Georgia 1795; Tattnall was educated in England before joining the U.S. Navy as a midshipman in 1812; he saw extensive action during the War of 1812 and participated in operations against the Barbary Pirates; promoted to lieutenant in 1818, he was assigned to Commodore David Porter's Mosquito Fleet for actions against pirates in the West Indies; while commanding the schooner *Grampus* in 1831, he captured a Mexican warship that had previously sacked an American vessel; after twenty-six years of almost continuous service at sea, Tattnall was stationed at the Boston Navy Yard from 1838 to 1847; following

brief service in the Mediterranean, he commanded the gunboat *Spitfire* during the Mexican War; thereafter he returned briefly to the Boston Navy Yard and commanded the *Saranac* in the Home Squadron; rising through the ranks to captain, he commanded the Pensacola Navy Yard from 1851 to 1854 and the *Independence* in the Pacific Squadron; in 1858 he assumed command of the East India Squadron and rendered valuable service in China; with Georgia's secession from the Union, he resigned his commission in February 1861; he became a captain and senior flag officer in the Georgia state navy and in March entered the Confederate States Navy as a captain; given command of the naval defenses of Georgia and South Carolina, he was unsuccessful in opposing the Federal capture of Port Royal in November 1861; selected to replace the wounded Franklin Buchanan in command of the Virginia defenses, including the ironclad *Virginia* (*Merrimac*), Tattnall, then in his fiftieth year of naval service, ordered the prized vessel destroyed when Norfolk was abandoned by the Confederates in May 1862; censured for this action, he requested a court-martial and was acquitted; deemed too old for continued sea duty, Tattnall was relegated to the command of shore defenses at Savannah; imprisoned after that city's fall, he was paroled in May 1865; after the war he removed to Nova Scotia but returned impoverished to Savannah in 1870, where he became port inspector, a position created for him by the city; he died there in 1871.

Tattnall proposed that the *Merrimac* try to capture the Yankee ironclad. The Rebel monster would engage her Union rival while Confederate seamen from the *Raleigh, Beaufort, Patrick Henry,* and *Jamestown* boarded the *Monitor,* disabled her turret, and blinded her vision. Once the Yankee ship had been crippled, she would be lashed to the smaller Confederate vessels and towed as a captive to Norfolk. Tattnall became convinced that this plan was the only way to defeat the Union ironclad. According to one seaman, he became obsessed with the idea, wandering around and muttering, "I will take her! I will take her if hell's on the other side of her!"

Early on the morning of April 11 the *Merrimac* and her consorts steamed to meet the Federal fleet in Hampton Roads. Tattnall longed for a chance at the *Monitor* but he found the ironclad and most of the other Federal warships anchored under the heavy guns of Fort Monroe. Three small transports were inside the entrance of Hampton Roads and were easily taken by the *Merrimac's* escorts. Tattnall knew, however, that he could not risk an attack against the *Monitor* while she was near the fort, so he tried unsuccessfully to lure the Union ironclad into a general engagement. Since the *Monitor* did not fall for the deception, Tattnall fired a final shot in this anticlimactic battle and retired to Norfolk. The *Merrimac* remained in the Elizabeth River without ever again confronting the *Monitor.* While no other combat occurred between the two vessels, the Rebel ironclad did exert tremendous influence over Federal strategy, ultimately forcing McClellan to alter his advance towards Richmond during the spring and summer of 1862.

McClellan's attack along the Peninsula ultimately forced General Joseph E. Johnston to evacuate Norfolk in early May. All stores and machinery at the Gosport Navy Yard that could be removed were evacuated; buildings and the dry dock were destroyed; meanwhile the *Merrimac* remained at Sewell's Point to divert Federal attention from the Confederate retreat. After consulting with his staff and army officers, Tattnall decided to lighten the ironclad's draft in an attempt to take the vessel up the James River to Richmond. But in the early morning hours of May 11, Tattnall learned that Federal forces had advanced on Norfolk. With a Yankee fleet in front at Hampton Roads and land forces to the rear in Norfolk, Tattnall knew that the *Merrimac* had to retreat or she would be captured. Much to his surprise, Tattnall discovered that even with a lightened draft his ironclad could not cross the sand bar at the mouth of the James River. His only recourse was to destroy the *Merrimac* to prevent her from falling into enemy hands.

The *Merrimac* steamed towards Craney Island where Tattnall ran the ship aground. For the next several hours, boats evacuated the more than three-hundred man crew. Catesby ap Roger Jones and John Taylor Wood prepared charges to fire the ship. Before getting into his boat, Lieutenant Littlepage sacrificed clothes from his knapsack to save the ironclad's banners and flags. Jones, the last to leave, set a match to a powder train and then rowed vigorously to shore. At about 5 A.M., as the ship's tired, hungry, and dejected crew set out on a twenty-two-mile march to Suffolk, the fire reached the *Merrimac*'s main magazine, which blew up with a deafening roar that rattled forests, towns, and villages for miles around. Tattnall sadly announced that "the *Virginia* no longer exists." The crew continued on their melancholy journey, arriving in Richmond the following day. From there they immediately marched to Drewry's Bluff to confront the approaching Federal fleet on the James River. Three days later, on May 15, Jones and the ship's crew, flying the tattered flags that Littlepage had saved, manned guns along the river and fired again at their old adversary.

Since its encounter with the *Merrimac* command of the *Monitor* had passed to Lieutenant William N. Jeffers, a twenty-two-year veteran and ordnance expert who had graduated from the Naval Academy in 1846 as a sixteen-year-old. During that spring engineer Stimers had repaired the ironclad's pilothouse while his fellow officers had pondered the role their ship would play in McClellan's forthcoming advance. After the fall of Norfolk, they learned that their ship and the ironclad *Galena*, accompanied by three wooden ships, would steam up the James River towards Richmond.

On Drewry's Bluff, eight miles downriver from Richmond, Confederate batteries waited until the Yankee ships were well within range before they began firing. For almost four hours Jones and the crew of the *Merrimac* mercilessly pounded the two Union ironclads in the river below. The Confederate shots did little damage to the *Monitor*, but they penetrated the *Galena*'s outer iron sides, seriously wounding her and forcing the two Union ships to retreat. In fact, this battle proved the experimental *Galena* a failure as an ironclad. The two battered and bruised vessels returned to Hampton Roads where the *Monitor* spent the remainder of the summer.

In early August the Federal ironclad received a new temporary commander, Thomas Stevens, while she underwent minor repairs and modifications. By September 11 John P. Bankhead, a forty-one-year-old South Carolinian who had remained loyal to the Union, assumed permanent command and took the *Monitor* to the Washington Navy Yard. Throughout October the ironclad underwent extensive renovations: retractable smokestacks and new life boats were fitted, and the dents patched with iron. Sailors were given a well-deserved furlough and the ship was opened to a curious public. By early November the *Monitor* was back on duty in Hampton Roads, where she remained until late December 1862.

Bankhead received orders on Christmas Day for the *Monitor* to proceed south to Beaufort, North Carolina, to assist with the blockade there, but bad weather delayed any departure until December 29. Once the ship finally departed all seemed well, but later that evening a gale blew in and the seas began to toss the little ship ruthlessly. During the next day the winds and waves rose, dashing across the ironclad and breaking against the turret and pilothouse. The *Monitor* was helpless, at the mercy of Mother Nature. Soon water began to flow in through the ship's many openings at a rate that the *Monitor*'s pumps could not handle. Crewmen reported that "water is gaining on us," as they desperately manned buckets. By 10:30 P.M., Bankhead reported to his escort, the U.S.S. *Rhode Island*, that he was in distress.

Aboard the ironclad, mechanical pumps and bucket brigades worked together as one, but the water continued to rise. The swell that had tossed the ship placed stress on the *Monitor*'s structure and produced cracks along the vessel's iron seams through which the water gushed. The packing around

John P. Bankhead: Born South Carolina 1821; the son of a War of 1812 and Mexican War army officer, Bankhead entered the U.S. Navy as a midshipman following his seventeenth birthday in 1838; he saw a variety of assignments on numerous vessels and earned promotion to lieutenant in 1852; although a Southerner by birth, Bankhead remained loyal to the Union during the Civil War; he served aboard the *Susquehanna* during the November 1861 capture of Port Royal

and commanded the *Pembina* and the *Florida* during operations against Fernandina, Florida, in May 1862; promoted to commander, he took charge of the ironclad *Monitor* after its famous battle with the C.S.S. *Virginia* (*Merrimac*); ordered to Beaufort, North Carolina, the *Monitor* foundered in bad weather off Cape Hatteras on the last day of 1862; despite the herculean efforts of Bankhead and his crew, the ironclad went down, taking several officers and men with it; Bankhead, who remained with his ship to the last, was pulled from the water to safety; he served throughout the remainder of the war and in 1866 was promoted to captain; he commanded the *Wyoming* in the East India Squadron until illness forced him to relinquish command; while returning to the United States in March 1867, Captain Bankhead died at sea near Aden, Arabia (Yemen).

the ship's turret had washed, allowing the water to rise quickly. Bankhead, giving up the battle, fought the monstrous waves on deck and signaled the *Rhode Island* to come alongside. Meanwhile, the rising water level inside the ship extinguished the boiler fires, rendering the ship's pumps ineffectual. Bailing parties continued work at a feverish pace but could not keep up with the water pouring in.

At last, boats from the *Rhode Island* came alongside to rescue the helpless seamen. One by one the crewmen inched across the unprotected deck, braving the swells that threatened to wash them away. Maneuvering their way into the lifeboats became another harrowing experience as several seamen fell overboard, never to be seen again. Some of the sailors clung desperately to the turret, refusing to take their chances with the rough seas. Captain Bankhead was the last to leave his vessel as he jumped into the chilly water. Crewmen pulled their commander into a lifeboat and rowed to safety. Ultimately four officers and twelve men chose to remain behind rather than seek refuge aboard the *Rhode Island*; they went down with the Union ironclad.

At about 1 A.M. on December 31, 1862, Bankhead, Paymaster Keeler, and others watched as the *Monitor's* running lights disappeared for the last time. Rescue boats that had returned to extricate the seamen clinging to the ironclad's turret found only an eddy "apparently produced by a sinking vessel." Ironically, the *Monitor* was almost within sight of land, about fifteen miles south of Cape Hatteras, North Carolina, when she sank. Unknown to those aboard the *Rhode Island*, when the ironclad foundered she rolled so that her turret touched the sandy bottom first and her hull rested on top. Regardless, Bankhead, Keeler, and others understood that "the *Monitor* is no more."

The two ships, the *Monitor* and the *Merrimac*, had introduced a revolution in naval technology because they demonstrated, without doubt, that wooden warships, regardless of their armaments, were no match for ironclad vessels. And although these two ships were very different in design, they both provided models for future Union and Confederate warships as well as for other nations. Even so, the problems associated with the *Merrimac*—slow speed, poor maneuverability, bad engines, and a lack of building materials—plagued the other twenty-two ironclads commissioned by the South during the war. The *Monitor*, with its low profile, high speed, and excellent maneuverability, became the basic model for some sixty future Yankee ironclads. But it would be quantity and not the individual features of the ships that determined the outcome of the war. The production capacity of the industrialized North gave it an advantage that paid great dividends. From 1863 to the end of the war almost every attack on Confederate ports featured ironclads in a major role; they served in Union operations in every river and harbor in the South. And while there would be other ironclad-to-ironclad engagements during the war, they, like the first between the *Monitor* and the *Merrimac*, also proved inconclusive.

As for John Lorimer Worden, after the battle he was taken to Washington, D.C., to recover. He met President Abraham Lincoln, who graciously honored him for the services he had rendered to the nation. In February 1863 Congress gave Worden a special vote of thanks and promoted him to captain. From October 1862 to June 1863 he commanded the ironclad *Montauk* in the South Atlantic Blockading Squadron, and participated in the Union attack on Charleston. He finished the war, blinded in one eye, as an inspector of ironclad construction. After the conflict he rose to the rank of rear admiral and served as the Superintendent of the Naval Academy (1869–74), commander of the European Squadron (1875–77) and member of the Navy's Examining and Retirement boards. He resigned in December 1886 and spent the remainder of his life at his Washington, D.C. home, where he died of pneumonia on October 18, 1897.

Confederate commander Franklin Buchanan was promoted to admiral in August 1862 for the "gallant and meritorious conduct" he had exhibited during the first day's battle. In August 1864, while commanding the Confederate naval flotilla at Mobile, Alabama, Buchanan fought his flagship *Tennessee* virtually single-handedly against David Glasgow Farragut's Union squadron. During the engagement, even though his other ships were disabled or driven to cover, Buchanan still courageously attacked without support. Wounded and captured, he remained a prisoner until exchanged in February 1865. After the war Buchanan became president of Maryland Agricultural College (1868–69), and secretary of the Mobile, Alabama, branch of the Life Insurance Company of America (1869–70). He retired to his home near Baltimore, where he died on May 11, 1874.

Catesby ap Roger Jones went on to command the ironclad *Chattahoochee* at Columbus, Georgia, and the naval works at Charlotte, North Carolina. Promoted to commander in 1863, he was soon transferred to the Confederate naval gun foundry and ordnance works at Selma, Alabama, where he remained until the end of the war. While at Selma, Jones demonstrated an ability to produce quality ammunition and guns that greatly benefited the Confederate war effort. In fact, Jones supplied the cannon at Fort Morgan in Mobile, and the guns for Buchanan's fleet in 1864. For about a year after the war, Jones, John M. Brooke, and Robert D. Minor formed a limited partnership that purchased American war material for foreign governments. This business took him to South America where several nations sought his ordnance expertise. While in Lima in 1866, Jones was hired by the Peruvian government, then at war with Spain. He was even supposedly offered command of a Peruvian naval squadron, but reportedly refused in deference to native officers.

After his brief stint in South America, Jones retired with his family to Selma. During his later years, he drafted for publication several accounts of the historic battle between the two ironclads. In spite of Jones's distinguished career as an ordnance specialist both before and after the War, the engagement between the *Monitor* and *Merrimac* became the defining moment of his life. For years afterwards, he received requests asking for his perspective on the historic engagement. Like so many others who participated, he told and retold the story, adding details about almost every aspect of the fight. It was ironic, however, that after living through such a monumental battle, Jones should have been mortally wounded, not by Union forces, but in a domestic dispute with his friend and neighbor J.A. Harral. The two men, although closely associated, had a quarrel and Harral shot Jones in the chest. On June 20, 1877, the former Confederate naval officer died.

The story of Jones, Buchanan, Worden, the *Monitor*, and the *Merrimac* is part of the much larger drama of the Civil War. But while many of the soldiers, seamen, and events of the conflict have been overshadowed or forgotten, those two days in early March 1862 remain etched in time. The *Monitor* and the *Merrimac* were revolutionary ships in a revolutionary battle, and those who fought in the engagement or witnessed it from shore soon realized that it was "one of the greatest naval engagements that has ever ocured [*sic*] since the Beginning of the world." But what separated this battle from so many others before was that iron and heavy guns made the difference. Even the editor of the Norfolk *Day Book*, who viewed the day's events with a critical eye, wrote that "this successful and terrible work will create a revolution in naval warfare, and henceforth iron will be king of the seas." A new age of technological warfare had begun.

APPENDIX A

Note: The information presented in the appendices is taken from *Official Records of the Union and Confederate Navies in the War of the Rebellion, Series I, Volume 1.*

FEDERAL FORCES

	Condition	Men	KIA	WIA	Guns
Congress	Sunk	434	120	16	50
Cumberland	Sunk	376	121		22
Minnesota	Damaged	550	6	20	40
Roanoke	Retreated	550		4	40
St. Lawrence	Damaged	480			50
Gunboats	3 Disabled	120	3	3	6
Forts	Silenced	200			20
Monitor	Not Damaged	57		1	2
	Total	2,890	250	44	230

The killed and wounded returns were taken from the report of Federal Fleet Surgeon William Maxwell Wood. They appear to be somewhat inaccurate.

APPENDIX B

CONFEDERATE FORCES

	Commander	Guns
Merrimac	Franklin Buchanan	12
Patrick Henry	John R. Tucker	12
Jamestown	I.W. Barry	2
Teaser	W.A. Webb	1
Beaufort	W.H. Parker	1
Raleigh	I.W. Alexander	1
Total		29

Wounded aboard *Merrimac*:	8
Killed aboard *Merrimac*:	2
Casualties aboard other vessels:	17
Total	27

APPENDIX C

OFFICERS ABOARD *MONITOR*

Flag Officer	John L. Worden
Executive Officer	Samuel D. Greene
Acting Master	Louis N. Stodder
Master's Mate	George Frederickson
Paymaster	William F. Keeler
Surgeon	Daniel C. Logue
Engineer	Alban C. Stimers
First Assistant Engineer	Isaac Newton

APPENDIX D

OFFICERS ABOARD *MERRIMAC*

Flag Officer   Franklin Buchanan

Executive Officer   Catesby ap Roger Jones

Lieutenants   Charles C. Simms
                                    R.D. Minor
                                    Hunter Davidson
                                    J. Taylor Wood
                                    J.R. Eggleston
                                    Walter Butt

Midshipmen   Fonte
                                    H.H. Marmaduke
                                    H.B. Littlepage
                                    Craig
                                    Long
                                    Roote
                                    V. Newton

Paymaster   James Semple

Surgeon   Dinwiddie B. Phillips

Assistant Surgeon   Algernon S. Garnett
                                    Bennett W. Green

Captain of Marines   Reuben Thom

Engineer   H. A. Ramsay

FURTHER READING

Allen, Oliver E. "'The Monitor is Mine!'" *Invention and Technology* 2 (1996): 35–42.

"Battle of Hampton Roads—Confederate Official Reports," *Southern Historical Society Papers* 7 (1879): 305–314.

Baxter, James P. *The Introduction of the Ironclad Warship.* Cambridge, Massachusetts: Harvard University Press, 1933.

Bennett, Frank M. *The Monitor and the Navy Under Steam.* Boston: Houghton, Mifflin and Company, 1900.

Brooke, John M. "The Plan and Construction of the *Merrimac*," *Southern Historical Society Papers* 19 (1891): 3–34.

_____. "The Virginia, or Merrimac: Her Real Projector," *Southern Historical Society Papers* 19 (1891): 3–34.

Butts, Francis B. "The Loss of the *Monitor*," *Battles and Leaders of the Civil War.* Vol. 1:745–748.

Cline, William R. "The Ironclad Ram Virginia—Confederate States Navy," *Southern Historical Society Papers* 32 (1904): 243–249.

Colston, Raleigh E. "Watching the *Merrimac*," *Battles and Leaders of the Civil War.* Vol. 1:712–714.

Cracknell, William H. *United States Navy Monitors of the Civil War.* Windsor, England: Profile Publications, 1973.

Davis, William C. *Duel Between the First Ironclads.* Baton Rouge: Louisiana State University Press, 1975.

Dew, Charles B. *Ironmaker to the Confederacy: John R. Anderson and the Tredegar Iron Works.* New Haven, Connecticut: Yale University Press, 1966.

Eggleston, John R. "Captain Eggleston's Narrative of the Battle of the Merrimac," *Southern Historical Society Papers* 41 (1916): 166–178.

Ericsson, John. "The Building of the *Monitor*," *Battles and Leaders of the Civil War.* Vol. 1:748–750.

Fowler, William M., Jr. *Under Two Flags: The American Navy in the Civil War.* New York: W.W. Norton and Company, 1990.

Gallagher, Gary. "'The Fight Between the Two Iron Monsters': The *Monitor* versus the *Virginia* as Described by Major Stephen Dodson Ramseur, C.S.A.," *Civil War History* 3 (1984): 268–271.

Greene, S. Dana. "I Fired the First Gun and Thus Commenced the Great Battle," *American Heritage* 7 (1957): 10–13, 102–105.

_____. "In the *Monitor* Turret," *Battles and Leaders of the Civil War.* Vol 1:719–729.

Jones, Catesby ap Roger. "Services of the *Virginia* (*Merrimac*)," *Southern Historical Society Papers* 1 (1876): 90–91.

Jones, Judge Lewis Hampton. *Captain Roger Jones, of London and Virginia.* Albany, New York: Joel Munsell's Sons, Publishers, 1891.

Jones, T. Catesby. "The Iron-Clad *Virginia*," *Virginia Magazine of History and Biography* 49 (1941): 297–303.

Littlepage, Hardin B. "*Merrimac* vs. *Monitor*: A Midshipman's Account of the Battle with the 'Cheeze-Box,'" in William C. King and William P. Derby, comps. *Camp-Fire Sketches and Battlefield Echoes of '61–65.* Springfield, Massachusetts: 1880.

Mabry, W.S. *Brief Sketch of the Career of Captain Catesby Ap R. Jones.* Selma, Alabama: Privately Printed, 1912.

MacBride, Robert. *Civil War Ironclads: The Dawn of Naval Armor.* Philadelphia: Chilton Books, 1962.

Martin, Charles, "Sinking of the *Congress* and *Cumberland* by the *Merrimac*," *Personal Recollections of the War of the Rebellion: Papers Read Before the New York Commandery, Military Order of the Loyal Legion of the United States.* ed., A. Noel Blakeman. New York: Knickerbocker Press, 1891–1912.

Newton, Virginius. "The Ram Merrimac," *Southern Historical Society Papers* 20 (1892):1–26.

Norris, William. "The Story of the Confederate States Ship *Virginia* (Once Merrimac)," *Southern Historical Society Papers* 42 (1917): 204–233.

O'Neil, Charles. "Engagement Between the *Cumberland* and the *Merrimack*, *United States Naval Institute Proceedings* 48 (1922): 863–893.

Phillips, Dinwiddie B. "The Career of the Merrimac," *The Southern Bivouac* 2 (1887): 598–608.

Ramsay, H. Ashton. "Interesting Data About the *Merrimac*," *Confederate Veteran* 16 (1908): xvii–xix.

_____. "Most Famous of Sea Duels: The *Merrimac* and *Monitor*," *Harper's Weekly*, 10 February 1912, 11–12.

Reaney, Henry. "How the Gun-Boat *Zoave* Aided the *Congress*" *Battles and Leaders of the Civil War*. Vol 1:714–715.

_____. "The Monitor and Merrimac," in *War Papers: Being Papers Read Before the commandery of the State of Michigan, Military Order of the Loyal Legion of the United States*. Detroit, 1893–1898, 2:167–172.

Scharf, J. Thomas., ed. *History of the Confederate States Navy*. New York: Rogers and Sherwood, 1887.

Selfridge, Thomas O., Jr. "The Merrimac and the Cumberland," *Cosmopolitan* 15 (1893): 176–184.

Stiles, Israel N. "The *Merrimac* and the *Monitor*," *Military Essays and Recollections: Papers Read Before the Illinois Commandery, Military Order of the Loyal Legion of the United States*. Chicago: A.C. McClurg and Company, 1891–1912.

Still, William N., Jr. *Iron Afloat: The Story of the Confederate Armorclads*. Nashville: Vanderbilt University Press, 1971.

Stimers, Alban C. "An Engineer Aboard the *Monitor*," ed., John D. Milligan, *Civil War Times Illustrated* 11 (1970): 28–35.

Stodder, Louis N. "Aboard the U.S.S. *Monitor*," ed. Albert S. Crockett, *Civil War Times Illustrated* 1 (1963): 31–36.

Stuyvesant, Moses S. "How the *Cumberland* Went Down," *War Papers and Personal Reminiscences, 1861–1865: Read Before the Commandery of the State of Missouri, Military Order of the Loyal Legion of the United States.* St. Louis: Becktold & Co., 1892.

Trexler, Harrison A. *The Confederate Ironclad Virginia (Merrimac).* Chicago: University of Chicago Press, 1938.

United States War Department. *War of the Rebellion: Official Records of the Union and Confederate Armies.* Washington: Government Printing Office, 1880–1901, 128 vols.

Welles, Gideon. *Diary of Gideon Welles, Secretary of the Navy Under Lincoln and Johnson*, ed., Howard K. Beale. New York: W.W. Norton and Company, Inc., 1960.

White, E.V. *The First Iron-Clad Naval Engagement in the World.* New York. J.S. Ogilvie Publishing Company, 1906.

Wilson, Herbert W. *Ironclads in Action: A Sketch of Naval Warfare from 1855 to 1895.* Boston: Little, Brown and Company, 1896.

Wingfield, J.H.D. "Thanksgiving Service on the *Virginia*, March 10, 1862," *Southern Historical Society Papers* 19 (1891): 248–251.

Wood, John Taylor. "The First Fight of Iron-Clads," *Battles and Leaders of the Civil War.* Vol. 1:692–711.

PHOTO CREDITS

We are grateful to the Naval Historical Foundation Photo Service, Washington Navy Yard, Washington, D.C., for the photograph of Alban C. Stimers, and for the pictures depicting an illustrative history of the *Monitor* and the *Merrimac* and the battle between the two ships.

We acknowledge the cooperation of the U.S. Army Military History Institute at Carlisle Barracks, Pennsylvania, for the photographs of John P. Bankhead, Franklin Buchanan, John A. Dahlgren, John Ericsson, Samuel Dana Greene, Matthew F. Maury, Thomas O. Selfridge, Joseph B. Smith, William B. Taliaferro, Josiah Tattnall, Gershom J. Van Brunt, Charles Wilkes, John Lorimer Worden, the officers aboard the *Monitor*, and the picture of the *Merrimac*.

The photograph of Stephen R. Mallory is from the National Archives.

The photograph of Gideon Welles is from Gideon Welles, *Diary of Gideon Welles*. Volume I. Boston: Houghton Mifflin, 1911.

The photograph of Catesby ap Roger Jones and the illustrations of the burning of the Frigate *Merrimac*, the *Merrimac* ramming the *Cumberland*, the explosion of the *Congress*, and the *Monitor* and *Merrimac* at close range are from *Battles and Leaders of the Civil War*. I. New York: Thomas Yoseloff, 1956.

INDEX